To Siegfried Schulz, PEC:
Enjoy & learn!

May 27th 2006.

Anecdotes of Would-be Experts

by

Arthur O. R. Thormann

Specfab Industries Ltd.
Edmonton, Alberta, Canada

Library and Archives Canada Cataloguing in Publication

Thormann, Arthur O. R. (Arthur Otto Rudolf), 1934-
Anecdotes of would-be experts / Arthur O.R. Thormann

ISBN 0-9685198-3-0

I. Title

PS8589.H54945A74 2004   C813'.54   C2004-904925-9

Publisher: Specfab Industries Ltd.
                    13559 - 123A Avenue
                    Edmonton, Alberta, Canada
                    T5L 2Z1
                    Telephone: 780-454-6396

2nd Printing: PageMaster Publication Services Inc.
                    10180 - 105 Street
                    Edmonton, Alberta, Canada
                    T5J 1E1
                    Telephone: 780-425-9303

Cover Design: Arthur O.R. Thormann

For Garett, Megan, Samantha, and Jordan

Contents

Main Characters:

Cliff Jensen – is the President and CEO of Belvue Industrial Constructors, a multinational construction company. He also chairs a Board Committee that determines the value and advisability of any proposed endeavors of Belvue's division heads.

Phil Potter – is one of Belvue's regional Vice Presidents. He is located in the same offices with Les Payne and is Les's immediate superior.

Les Payne – is one of Belvue's Operational Managers. He is in charge of all operations of Belvue's Midwest Division.

1

Phil's Folly

Phil told me to close the door as I walked into his office Monday morning. "How's your estimate coming?" he asked as I sat down.

"Which estimate? We're working on five right now."

"The one for the PetroHi-G upgrader," he said.

"Okay, I think, but it's slow-going – the engineering is lousy!"

"That could be an advantage later," he said, "lots of extras to pay for shortcomings, you know." Phil's sales background left a substantial gap in his understanding of production losses that usually occur due to disruptions by extras caused to the remainder of unfinished work. We've had these discussions before to no avail.

"It could also be detrimental," I pointed out, "causing us plenty of unwanted disruptions and delays nobody's willing to pay for."

He looked at me for a few seconds and then said, "It'll be part of a claim, Les, a legitimate claim! It'll be up to our lawyers to collect on it. Not our fault if they don't." It was my turn to look at him for a few seconds. Everything in construction was simple for Phil, mainly because he didn't understand it, or didn't want to understand it. He just refused to acknowledge the complexities. His sales background, I guessed. "You know damn well we need this project to meet our budget forecast," he added. I didn't say anything – what's the use?

Then I asked, "Is there anything else, Phil?"

"There is," he said. "You've prepared a revised completion

forecast for head office on the transit project." I nodded. "Your revised forecast lowered our estimated profit to zero." I nodded again. "This makes things very awkward for me," he said.

"Can't be helped, Phil, the estimate was short in several areas. Even at zero percent profit, my forecast is optimistic."

"Couldn't you have postponed the bad news for a month, until after the year end?" he asked in an accusing tone.

"You know darn well that head office won't tolerate such a delay, Phil. They'll accuse me of withholding vital information. I hope you'll remember Cliff's warning at our last meeting." Cliff is the president of the company, but instead of talking to Phil, his vice president for this region, he preferred to give me, his operations manager, a hard time. Probably, he excused Phil's sales background.

"For Christ's sake, Les," he yelled, "how would they possibly know when you discovered the discrepancy?" I looked at him again for a while, although I knew he meant every word of what he was saying. He was my immediate superior, but head office still blamed me for tardy information, not him, and they had uncanny ways of finding out the truth. Besides, it was against my upbringing to deceive people.

"Are you ordering me to withhold this information from head office, Phil?" I immediately regretted this question. It implied that I would follow his orders even knowing that they were wrong and that head office would strongly disapprove.

"You know I'm not!" he yelled again, "I'm only suggesting you delay it for a while!"

"But I would have to turn in a deceiving, falsified forecast," I said. "Our purchase records wouldn't even support it, Phil." He gave me another long, suspicious look, like the one you give a suspected traitor.

I finally asked, "Is that all, Phil?"

"That's all," he said quietly, giving me a sad look. I closed the door on my way out.

§

Later, Deb, his secretary, confided in me that Phil had changed my forecast before sending it off to head office. Even she was shocked – because the forecast was over my signature – although she was used to Phil's methods by now. The profit margin was back to six percent. Nevertheless, he was too much of a coward to initial the changes he made, thus making it appear that I had made them.

Phil Potter and I didn't always have a strained relationship. Two years earlier, when our revenue comfortably exceeded our budget forecast and most of our projects showed a tidy profit, he and I often went for a drink after work. Phil drank double martinis. Ordering fewer drinks gave the appearance that he drank less. I stuck to wine – preferably lower percentage white wines. Our discussions were seldom about personal issues. Phil liked to expand on his dreams of high revenues and profits. I helped him by passing on every rumor I came across of new and bigger mega-projects. Size never discouraged Phil. It only meant more supervision and a larger workforce.

There we sat, in a dark lounge, spinning bigger and better yarns with each new drink. The problem was, Phil remembered most of it the next day and got me working on the fulfillment of his dreams. This meant that I had to travel all over the country and convince construction owners and engineering companies of our ability to perform and the value to them to put us on their bid lists. Phil never took "no" for an answer. When I was unsuccessful convincing these people, he would visit them himself, and lie a little, if need be.

Of course, we didn't make all grades, but our success ratio was high enough to satisfy Phil. I had no idea how we would build all the construction we were asked to bid on. But, often, our competitors came to my aid, bidding the projects too low to attract Phil's desire to beat them. His craving for higher profits always got the better of him. We would then guzzle some drinks again, expounding on the likelihood of one or another competitor going bankrupt.

In retrospect, these were not bad times. Bad times started when Phil made us cut costs – he wouldn't even hear of cutting profit, lecturing us that this would be the fastest way of going out of business. But we seldom realized the costs he convinced us to cut, especially as far as labor costs were concerned. I wondered, often, how Phil had acquired the knowledge about labor costs he tried to convey to us. There was no use arguing with him – he may not have always been right, but he was always the boss. So, we just sat there in awe, watching him do his thing. We took solace in the belief that he would take responsibility should his cost-cuts not work out. Wrong again! When labor costs, for example, ran over the budget, Phil would call in our supervisors and severely chastise them.

Afterwards, as we sat again in the lounge over drinks, he would speculate on the value of these failing supervisors. I reminded him that they may be trying the impossible, considering his cost chopping, but he would tolerate no excuses – they knew the amount of money they had available and should have the smarts to bring the costs in within the estimate. After all, wasn't he doing the same as far as his budget was concerned? I didn't mention to him that he established his own budgets and massaged the figures whenever they showed signs of weakness. He sighed. "No, believe me, Les, these supervisors don't have what it takes!"

I didn't have long to wait for head office to respond to my forecasts. Thursday morning, Deb stuck her head into my office and said, "Cliff Jensen's on line two for you, Les," with a meaningful look in her eyes. I waited a full minute before picking up the receiver.

"Hello," I said.

"Les? It's Cliff. How are you?"

"I'm fine. How about you, Cliff?"

"I'm fine, too. How's it going?" – his first loaded question. Cliff is as sharp as a tack. I often wondered about that. He has a slight French accent. He told me once that his French mother insisted on his learning French before English when he was a boy.

"As well as can be expected under the circumstances," I replied.

"What circumstances?" He shot back.

I knew I was getting deeper into the quagmire by the minute. "Well, we're having difficulties with some of our projects. On one of them, we may even end up with a claim." Normally, the word "claim" would sharpen all his senses. This time he ignored it.

"Which project gives you the most difficulties?" he asked.

I knew there was no way out of it now. If I didn't tell him the truth now, he would know in a month that I had been lying. "The transit project," I said.

"That's strange!" he shot back. "I thought you had resolved your difficulties on that project."

I wondered how far into our division his spy network reached. There was Jean-Luc, our controller, of course. Phil told me a few times that Jean-Luc is a head office spy. But Jean-Luc had his head buried in paperwork all day, and his ability to forecast the future by merely studying paper would be very limited. Everyone in the division gave him only information on a need-to-know basis. Rather than Jean-Luc, I had a suspicion that Deb wasn't as loyal to Phil as he liked to believe.

"What gave you that idea?" I asked innocently.

"Your forecast," he said. "First you brought the profit down to zero, then you struck out the figures and brought the profit back up to six percent."

"I don't remember doing that," I said. "As far as I am concerned, the profit is still at zero."

He was silent for a minute. "I'm coming out," he said finally. "I have to go over next year's budget with you and

5

Phil anyway."

"It's pretty close to Christmas, Cliff. When would you be coming?"

"You're not taking holidays before Christmas?" It was more a statement than a question.

"No, no," I said, "but you may find it hard to get a seat on a flight in this Christmas rush."

"I'll come early next week, he said. "I'll let Phil know when, after I make the arrangements."

"See you next week, then," I said. "Have a good flight."

"Yeah, thanks." The line went dead.

I wasted no time seeing Phil to apprise him of my conversation with Cliff, and Cliff's decision to come out the following week. Phil was unhappy. He had planned to get away early for Christmas.

The Christmas activities in the week before Christmas should have put me in a better mood. Instead, my mind was full of gloom and doom. I knew that when Cliff meets with us I would either cut my own throat or Phil's – neither prospect was too appealing. I was still hoping that Cliff wouldn't be able to get a flight out, but that would only delay the evil day.

I was late getting into the office on Monday. Cliff was already there, chatting with Phil. He had caught a flight out on the weekend.

"Make yourself available at ten o'clock," said Phil, and closed his door.

I tried to keep myself busy, but my mind was in Phil's office. I was imagining the things Phil might say to Cliff to gain favor. At ten, I took my coffee into the meeting room. Phil and Cliff were already spread out at the conference table, looking at graphs and spreadsheets – Phil's proposed budget, no doubt.

Cliff looked up and said, "Sit down, Les. Sit down." He talked to Phil for another two minutes and then turned to me.

"I need to straighten out your forecast for the transit

6

project," he said. "You crossed out some figures without initialing them, and I need to know which figures are correct."

I looked at my forecast sheet and said, "I did not cross out these figures; the crossed out figures are correct."

He took the sheet from me, looked at it intensely, and said, "Who, then, crossed out these figures?" I had the strangest feeling he knew darn well who crossed out the figures but couldn't admit it without revealing his source; he probably hoped that I would point the finger.

I said, "I don't know, Cliff." This was partially true, since my information was based on hearsay.

Cliff pretended to study the figures some more. Then he turned to Phil and me and said sternly, "Let's get one thing straight: It is folly for anyone to try to deceive me. One way or another, the truth has a way of coming out. I won't make a further issue of this, but if it happens again heads are going to roll. You two are responsible here, and it should be your concern who in this division alters the figures in your reports. You, Phil, are responsible for the yearly budgets, and you, Les, are responsible for the monthly cost forecasts. You two can get together to discuss each other's reports, but you must reach a consensus if you wish to make any changes. Do I make myself clear?" He looked back and forth at each of us.

"Okay by me," I said.

"Yes," mumbled Phil.

"Good," said Cliff. "Now let's go over next year's budget before we leave for the club to find out what's on their menu for Christmas lunch."

2

Phil's Auction Loss

My Saturdays were family days, but occasionally I went to the office for two or three hours to catch up on a hectic week. When I entered the office on this particular Saturday, Phil was brooding over a set of specifications.

I said, "Hello! You look busy."

He looked up and smiled – a good sign! He said, "I've just got an idea how we can land our budget revenue for the next three years." His normally pale complexion was slightly flushed – another good sign. He poked his nose into the specs again.

"Are you going to let me in on it?" I asked accusingly.

He looked up again and said, "Here, take a look for yourself," and handed me the specs.

I scanned the first two pages of the Instructions to Bidders section and said, "Too big for us, Phil; besides, the locals will get first crack at it, you know that!"

"No, they won't," he said. "We're pre-qualified by the owners, and that means, we're as good as the locals!"

I gave him a doubtful look. We were talking about six bid packages for the construction of grain terminals, all to be bid separately in succession, with an option to combine each new package with any number of packages bid previously.

"Even if we think we can handle this size of project, we're sure to have difficulties putting together an effective workforce. It's strange territory for us, and the local unions won't bend over backwards either to help us," I said.

"I'm not concerned about that," he replied. "We have ten good supervisors that we can send in to handle the workforce for us."

I thought about it for a minute. He was right in some respects, and I didn't want to throw more cold water on his enthusiasm. Besides, it was catching. I started to get excited. The project would certainly be the biggest challenge I've ever faced.

"How do you intend to handle the bidding?" I said. "It sounds like an auction to me, judging by the instructions to bidders."

"It is, it is!" he exclaimed. "Don't you see what an advantage this presents us with?"

I must have been slightly on the dull side that morning, because I said, "Run me through the procedure, will you, please, Phil?"

"Well," he said, "we'll bid the first tender package high, to find out where the competition sits, and to deceive them as to our real intent. They'll think we're not really interested. We'll also bid all subsequent tender packages high, but we'll reduce each combined package slightly – this is only logical because of some reduced costs – except the last bid combining all tender packages. We'll bid that one at our lowest possible markup. That way, we'll end up with the entire project – all six tender packages!" He smiled at me with a sly look on his face.

I was astonished. "You really mean that you're willing to gamble all or nothing, Phil?"

"Exactly," he said.

"Think of the enormous costs involved, just to prepare the tenders and to make the required site visits," I complained.

"It'll be worth it, Les," he said, "I'm sure we'll end up with this project, according to my tender strategy."

I sat silently for another minute. "Phil," I said finally, "I have bad experience playing games with combined packages. I was always more successful bidding my lowest price for each tender package. Sure, I may not end up with all of them, but I'm certain to end up with one or two."

9

"That's just it, Les," he said, "Your competitors will have had the same experience and will bid their best price for each package." He gave me another sly smile. "Don't you see? We'll know exactly where they sit on all but the last package, and we'll be able to put together one final combination for all tender packages based on that knowledge!" He grinned at me as if he'd just figured out how to commit the perfect crime.

During the next few months, I was unbelievably busy. We utilized seven estimators to work on the various disciplines. Phil even insisted that our supervisors familiarize themselves with the project – he was that sure of landing it. Of course, he left all the organizational and instructional tasks, and the various mandatory site visits, up to me. In the meantime, he sat behind his desk and worked out future budgets based on having this project. Each time we closed another tender package, I reminded him of the benefit of landing just one or two of these. He was not interested. "We'll get them all!" he assured me.

But I could not shake my ominous feeling. I knew some of our competitors – smart fellows, all of them – they had surely figured out by now what our game might be. Each time a new tender package closed, we submitted a new combined price for all packages bid, and this combined price came closer and closer to the sum of the various bidders' low tender prices. When I mentioned my concerns to Phil, he just laughed and said, "It doesn't matter, Les. Not one of them is in a position to bid a lot price for all six tender packages! The owners have really played into our hands with this bidding procedure."

He was very logical, and I could not think of any arguments to counter him. So, I continued to have our crews work on these tender packages as diligently as possible. Each time I attended a tender opening, I kept track of all bids and any alternate proposals. After five tender packages were bid, there were five different contractors with low package prices. Alarmingly, the sum of their low bids was already lower than

10

our estimated cost. I couldn't see how Phil would possibly arrive at a lower price for our combined package. I showed Phil my figures after the fifth tender package closed, and he frowned for the first time. Then he told me, "The last tender package includes most of the instrumentation; this gives us a decided advantage." However, so far, we were not low bidder on any of the tender packages – not even on any of our combined prices for tender packages.

Our estimators were well into the last tender package when Phil received a registered letter from the owners' prime consultant:

> We regret to have to inform you that due to pressure from local contractors to spread the work as widely as possible, the owners have decided against accepting tenders for combined tender packages and will award contracts based on the low tender for each tender package. We are sorry for any inconvenience this may have caused you.

Phil called me on the intercom and requested my presence in his office straight away. He pushed the letter across his desk as I sat down.

I had barely scanned it as he shouted, "They can't do this! We based our whole bidding strategy on their original Instructions to Bidders! We'll sue!"

I had never seen him so livid – his normally pale face was actually red – as his eyes threw daggers at me, as if I were responsible.

I decided against an immediate response. After a few moments, I said, "Suing them is a waste of time and money. The specs make it very clear that they don't have to accept the lowest or any tender."

"That's not the point!" he shouted. "They have deceived us and have caused us a lot of extra work for nothing!"

I could not reason with him in his present state of mind, so I suggested that we discuss our next move over a drink after work. It took two double martinis for him to calm down a little. I decided, now is the time.

"Phil, you said yourself that we have a big advantage on the last tender package," I said, gently. "So, let's submit our best price for this package and be satisfied with it. After all, it is the largest package of the lot."

"No way!" he said, "I don't deal with deceitful people! Tomorrow, we'll roll up the drawings and return them!"

"You mean you're going to lose your last chance to get a package of this project – the best package of this project?"

"You got that right!" he said. And that was his last word on this subject.

3

Phil Wants an Opinion

It was one of those rainy Saturdays that prevented most leisure activities, and I decided to spend a couple of hours at the office to catch up on my work. I stuck my head into Phil's office to say "hello" and found him in a glum mood.

"Anything wrong?" I asked.

He looked at me absentmindedly and shrugged his shoulders. I decided to leave him be and proceeded to my office. Half an hour later, he walked past my office and came back with a cup of coffee.

"What're you busy at?" he said listlessly.

"I'm finalizing some monthly forecasts for head office," I said.

"Goddamn waste of time," he remarked.

I didn't argue and continued with my work. In his present mood, I knew there was little I could say to cheer him up.

"Why don't you grab a cup of coffee and come to my office?" he said finally. Maybe he didn't feel much like sitting there, watching me work.

As I sat down across from him, he mumbled, "Goddamn Bill Cawlick."

I gave him an astonished look. Bill was the only one of our project managers who occupied the position of Phil's protégé. In fact, Bill should have reported to me on the Refinery Project, but Phil had insisted that he'll look after it himself.

"I don't think Bill has played it straight with me," he continued.

I stayed mum. I knew Bill couldn't be trusted to reveal problems on his projects.

"I had a call from his wife last night," said Phil. "She told me Bill's in the hospital for observation."

"What's wrong with him?"

"Don't know. She said he was acting strangely. Might be a nervous breakdown."

"He seemed okay to me on Wednesday," I said.

"Hell, if it's genuine, it can happen from one minute to the next. But I don't think it's genuine," he added, "I think he's pretending."

"Why? For heaven's sake!" I exclaimed.

Phil gave me an appraising look. "I think he's lost control of the Refinery Project," he said. "I think the job's got to big for him, and he wants out!"

It was my turn to give him an appraising look. "You must have something to go on to make these statements," I said.

"Just a few little things that don't make sense – and a gut feel," he said sadly. "I want you to head out there on Monday," he added after a while. "Take a close look around, and talk to a few people."

"Bill won't like it, I said.

"Bill is in no position to object," he countered. "I have to know how bad it is," he added.

I didn't ask him why he's not heading out to the project himself. With his background, I knew he wouldn't know what to look for, or what questions to ask.

"You'll have to clear it with the site," I said, "I mean let our supervisors know I'm acting on your instructions."

"Don't worry," he said. "It'll probably take you most of the day. I'll wait here for you to come back."

I spent a good part of Saturday going over the plans and specs to prepare myself for Monday. The entire project seemed to consist of structural steel, vats, pumps, trays, and controls – hundreds of them. Even long after I left the office, I couldn't get the project out of my mind.

I was glad when Monday morning came and I was heading

out of town. My previously issued I.D. got me past the project gate in less than five minutes. Our site office was already like a beehive. Supervisors and foremen were discussing the details of the day. I poured myself some coffee and pretended to study the site plan that covered most of the east wall. Nobody paid any attention to me. After most of our people had cleared out, Tom, our superintendent, joined me.

"Sorry. Monday-morning details," he said.

"I'm the one who's sorry," I said, "I should have come out on another day." He didn't disagree.

"What's on your mind?" he asked politely.

"The project is nearly 75% complete," I said. "Head office is insisting on personal verifications of my forecasts at this stage." May as well give my visit an official status, I decided. If I had to get rough to find out the truth, I could always blame it on head office.

"Who said the project is 75% complete?" he asked, "Phil?"

"No, I'm just going by our budget expenditure."

"That's a joke," he laughed. "You don't mean Billy-boy's rotten budget figures?"

"What's wrong with them?" I asked innocently.

"You couldn't build an outhouse in your backyard with Billy's budget figures!" he complained.

"I haven't heard of any budget shortages."

"That's because you're listening to the wrong people." Tom grinned. I didn't pursue this.

"Let's have a look around," I said. As he started his four-by-four, I asked, casually, "What's your project-completion assessment, Tom?"

"Sixty percent – max!" he said promptly.

"If you're right, we could lose quite a bundle," I said.

"Have already lost it!" he snorted. I didn't pursue this either.

"Could you stop for a moment at the owners' project office?" I said. "I want to say 'hello' to Trevor."

"He doesn't like us much," he replied. "I'll wait in the truck for you."

I asked the receptionist if Mr. Trenton is free to see me for a minute. "I'll check," she said. "Who shall I say is calling?" I gave her my name. Trevor is a good project manager. He and I went back a ways, and I was sure he'd make time for me. Trevor is also as straight a shooter as they come. A few years ago, he helped me out of a jam. I still feel indebted to him.

"Go right in," she said. "He's expecting you."

"Hi, Les!" Trevor said as he got out of his chair to shake my hand. "What brings you to our neck of the woods?"

"Phil wants me to check on things," I replied.

"Little late in the day, isn't it?" he shot back.

"Late for what?" I asked innocently.

"Late for remedies, that's what!" He gave me a stern look.

"What remedies? C'mon Trevor!"

"I'll give it to you straight:" he said, "You've got rotten supervision out here!" I looked at him in disbelief. "It's true!" he added.

"Could you be more specific, Trevor?"

"Sure. I'll give you a good example: Your crews ran control lines to where power lines should go, and none of your supervisors caught it!"

"You're kidding me."

"Wish I were," he said quietly. "It's already shoved our completion date out of sight!" I looked him straight in the eyes for a moment. He nodded. "And to add insult to injury," he added, "your fair-haired boy Bill is threatening us with a delay claim! I guess he doesn't know me very well: We have already prepared our delay claim against your company. Our legal beagles are looking it over right now," he sneered.

My mind was racing. I knew Trevor wasn't engaging in idle talk. "What can I do to straighten this mess out?" I asked earnestly.

"Get some experienced supervision out here, for starters," he said, "and double shift, if necessary, to bring the schedule back on track."

I thanked him and got up. At the door, I turned around. "Oh, by the way," I said, "you keep pretty good track of our installations." He nodded. "Do you mind telling me your estimate of our project-completion percentage?"

"Not at all! 57%."

"Thanks again, Trevor. You'll be hearing from me."

I spent the rest of the day with Tom. We drove from one part of the site to another, and I took every opportunity to talk to individual crews. By the end of the day, I had a fairly good idea of the mess we were in, but no idea of how we might dig our way out of it.

Over lunch, I asked Tom why our supervisors hadn't caught the control line switch. "Easy enough mistake," he shrugged. "The lines all start from the same place, and they're all the same size. Our supervisors just didn't look for it, I guess. But the problem is blown way out of proportion. There were only half a dozen lines involved, and it didn't take too long to correct them."

After discussing a few options with Tom, I headed back to town. It was after seven when I arrived at the office. Phil was still waiting for me.

"Well?" he said, as I walked in.

"I wish it were well, Phil. I wish it were!"

I gave him a brief outline of my findings and my conversation with Trevor. Phil listened patiently without interrupting.

When I finished, he said quietly, "And what's your opinion?"

I just looked at him for a while, wondering what was going through his mind. I thought my report made the required action very clear. "I think we should follow Trevor's advice," I said.

"Like hell, we will!" he shot back. "Can't afford to!" He fumbled with some papers on his desk while I waited for more explanations. Finally, he said, "Head office still thinks we're making a profit on this project, and I won't be the one to disappoint them!"

"Phil," I said, "you haven't got a choice! If we're going to avoid serious delays on this project, and a hefty delay claim from the owners, I might add, we'll have to take Trevor's advice!"

"For your information," he said, "Bill has already started on a delay claim of his own. And that'll be the only way we'll cover our asses at head office! Do you read me?"

"Phil, you can't be serious," I said lamely. "We'll lose millions going that route!"

"Correction, Les. Our delay claim will lose millions. Wouldn't be the first or the last time that happened! Not much we can do about it either."

I sat there like a wet poodle. "Well," I said finally, "I better head home. It's almost ten o'clock." I didn't even say "good night" as I left him.

4

Phil Likes Bad Designs

Five of us were busy in the meeting room since seven in the morning finalizing a tender for a major upgrader. With me were my chief estimator, my chief purchaser, the prospective project manager, and a supervisor experienced in this type of construction.

We had gone over the estimate with a fine-toothed comb and made a few adjustments. We had also discussed each item of project overhead and agreed on the amounts and duration. The time was nearing 11:30 a.m. when we discussed an adjustment factor for potential disruptions due to the poor design. Just then, Phil joined us.

"How's it going, guys?" he asked. I told him that we were discussing the effect of the incomplete design on our work and our construction schedule:

"Disruptions, delays, accelerations, that sort of thing, you know," I said.

"I wouldn't worry too much about that," said Phil.

"We can't get away from the adverse effect on our work, Phil," I told him.

"I know," he countered. "We'll just have to file a claim for that. Knowing about it in advance is actually an advantage. We'll keep better track of the disruptions and delays from the outset." He gave me a challenging look. "I actually like bad designs," he added. "They can often be very profitable for contractors."

"Are you suggesting, Phil," I said, "that we just ignore the cost effects of the poor design?"

"Yes," he said.

Here we go again, I thought. Later, he'll no doubt blame our supervisors for production losses – claim or no claim. Just to be on the safe side, I increased two other job factors to offset for the missing poor-design factor. However, when we landed the project, I realized that I could have allowed more, judging by the difference between our tender and the next bidder's.

The project proceeded as I had expected, that is, we had steady production losses – mostly because of disruptions from all the change orders required for incomplete and faulty designs. Phil took an unusual interest in this project right from the outset. I suspected he felt a little guilty. Nevertheless, he blamed our supervisors for the constant production losses, and he didn't miss any opportunities to ask more questions, although he received copies of our weekly field-progress reports.

One Friday night when we were relaxing over drinks, Phil asked me how our preparations for a delay claim were coming.

"For the upgrader?" I enquired.

"Are there any other projects for which you're preparing delay claims?" he wanted to know.

"No," I said.

"Well, then?"

"Well, we're giving the required notices, but our intentions are not well received," I said.

"Are you allowing for production losses in your quotes for extras?" he wanted to know.

"We tried that, but it was rejected by the owners," I said.

"May be just as well," he said, "because any negotiated amount beforehand never covers the experienced amount, in the end."

I didn't say anything. I knew he was right. A few years back, I had negotiated a fixed percentage to be added to direct labor costs for anticipated production losses, and I found out, sadly, that even double this percentage would not have been enough.

"Better to give your notices, keep track of everything, and submit your claim at the completion of construction," he continued.

"I still have a strange feeling we'll lose out," I complained.

"Keep a positive outlook," he said, "or they'll smell your weakness!"

"I know," I replied. "I do! But you know what I mean."

He ignored this. "What are you doing to mitigate the effects?" he asked.

"It's hard to mitigate anything, Phil," I said. "There are just too many change orders that keep fouling things up. We no sooner learn to cope with one, and another one comes along."

"Well, at least we're getting our markups for overheads and profit on these change orders," he said with a sigh.

"But those markups don't pay for our production losses," I replied.

"No," he said, "the claim will look after these."

I was silent again. I just couldn't shake my nagging doubt. I was wondering, silently, why we didn't get any objections to our notices.

When supervisors prepare for a claim, they usually look more critically at all aspects of the project. They know they may be called upon to testify, so they're more apt to dot the i's and cross the t's. The increased awareness of the causes and effects will often help to reduce claims and could even eliminate them. This is, in itself, a form of mitigation, and it took place at the upgrader. Our supervisors' actions were as much to prevent production losses as they were to keep track of those that occurred. In the end, our claim wasn't nearly as extensive as I had originally anticipated.

After completion of construction, we spent two weeks finalizing the claim. Phil looked it over critically and gave us the nod. He signed the letter accompanying the claim submission. The letter briefly outlined the difficulties we had experienced and expressed the hope for an amicable settlement of our claim.

We didn't get an immediate response, and Phil began to show signs of nervousness. He wanted me to phone the owners' representative to find out what the hold-up might be. I talked him out of this, pointing out that it would look like a sign of weakness if we showed impatience too soon. He agreed – for a while.

Then, a few days later, he started again. I proposed to discuss a plan after work over drinks with him. He didn't waste much time after he took the first gulp of his double martini. "How do we handle their silence?" he asked. I had the impulse to say, "With silence," but I just shrugged my shoulders.

"You'll have to call them, Les."

"And say what?" I asked.

"Well, enquire if they've received the claim – they haven't even acknowledged it!"

"No need to acknowledge it, Phil," I said. "We couriered it. Remember?"

"Well, ask them if we can clarify any of its aspects."

I thought about this. "No," I said. "The claim document couldn't be clearer."

He knew this was true. "Well," he said, "ask them if they have a problem with it, goddamn it!"

I thought about this, too. "Phil," I said, "I don't want to put ideas in their heads."

"Okay," he said, "tell them head office wants us to settle this claim so that it won't appear in their next financial statement."

"That might work," I said. "I'll call them tomorrow morning."

Phil was satisfied. He visibly relaxed as he ordered his next double martini.

Next morning, I phoned Howard Sheldon, the owners' project manager. Howard and I had had a good relationship for a few years – strictly business, though, nothing personal.

"How's it going, Les?" he said. "What can I do for you?"

"Head office wants to know how close we are to settling our claim with you," I said. "They don't want to mention it in their next financial statement."

"There is no claim as far as we're concerned," he said flatly.

I thought quickly. What was he getting at? I hoped that this wasn't going to be one of those unreasonable denials. "I think we've provided enough detail of cause and effect," I said lamely.

"You did that," he replied. "We have no argument with your detail."

"Then what's the problem?" I asked.

"You have no entitlement."

"C'mon, Howard," I shot back. "You know the designs were lacking everywhere!"

"We know that, Les," he said patiently, "but you knew that, too, prior to submitting your tender, or you should've known!"

So that was it. This explained their complacent attitude toward our notices. My mind was spinning. I was wondering if they may be more receptive to a different approach or if their answer was final.

"Can we discuss this over lunch, Howard?" I asked hopefully.

"I've got to eat somewhere, but I'm not promising anything. It may well turn out to be a waste of your time and money."

"I'll take my chances," I said, with relief.

"Okay," he said, "call me next Monday for a date. My time this week is pretty well shot."

"I'll call you."

He told me to say "hello" to Phil and hung up.

I wasted no time bringing Phil into the picture.

"We'll sue," he said. "We've got a very good case!"

"Let me finish my negotiations with Howard first, Phil. Howard is not unreasonable, as you know."

"Well, he's sure unreasonable now!" he raised his voice.

I knew there was no use talking to him when he got himself into a stew. "We'll see next week," I replied.

He just glared at me as if to say, you're to blame for this development.

Come next Monday, I wasted no time calling Howard. I caught him in a good mood – he may have had a successful fishing trip on the weekend.

"I can make lunch on Thursday; bring deep pockets," he said and laughed.

I told him I would pick him up and take him to the club.

"Look forward to it," he said, and hung up.

Phil was unhappy about another three days' delay, of course.

Thursday was a rainy day, and I wasn't looking forward to a muddy jobsite. But Howard's secretary came to the rescue. She phoned me to enquire if I would mind picking up Howard at his office in town. "Glad to," I said with relief. The club was filled for lunch, but I had arranged for a table in a quiet corner. The talk centered on trivial things, at first. Howard complained that he still had some paving to complete, and the rain didn't help things. I bided my time through lunch and broached the subject over coffees.

"Howard, I was thinking about what you said last week," I finally said. "There's truth in it, but the required changes were more extensive than anyone could've anticipated."

"No more than on any other fast-track project, I venture."

"Well, we think it is. Most fast-track projects have incomplete designs, yes," I said, "but this project also had a lot of corrective designs."

He nodded. "But you must have known that, too, at the tender stage," he said.

"It's never easy to assess the full extend of this problem,

Howard," I replied. "If we did, we'd never land a job!"

"You mean, you only land jobs by underestimating the conditions?" he asked with a smile.

"Of course not!" I shot back. "I meant jobs with poor designs!"

He nodded again. I had the feeling that he was playing with me. He may very well have some settlement in mind, but his demeanor was neutral. I decided to change tack.

"Howard," I said, "we've done our best to finish the project on time and to mitigate the effects of the bad design. And our workmanship remained impeccable throughout construction, I might add."

He nodded again. "I know that, Les," he said, "and that's why we're going to reconsider." He paused for a few seconds then continued, "We're going to do our own assessment of what we think is fair and get back to you. Don't get your hopes up too high, but we'll offer you some compensation."

I dropped him off and rushed back to the office. Phil jested about my long "banker's lunch" but listened patiently to my report. "I don't think we should take a hat-in-hand approach," he said finally. "Our case is far too strong for that!"

I didn't feel like arguing with him. Instead, I said, "It can't hurt to find out what they have to offer."

He nodded his agreement.

We had to wait another two weeks before Howard called me to say that their response was on the way over by courier. It arrived mid-afternoon. Phil read it and then handed it to me. The letter was short: First, a statement that the owners admitted no responsibility for our production loss. Second, some praise of our quality control and recognition that we maintained the schedule under adverse circumstances. Last, because of our satisfactory performance and the owners' desire to keep us on their bid list, an offer of fifty percent of our claim on a "Without Prejudice" basis, with an acceptance time limit of ten days. I looked up at Phil.

He'd put on his grumpy look and said, "We'll sue, of course!"

"I don't think that's wise, Phil."

"And why not, may I ask?"

"Well, for one thing, the legal costs are too high."

"And for another thing?" His look told me that he was half agreeing with me.

"And for another thing," I said, "we would have to produce our estimate and our cost records in evidence."

"What's wrong with that?" he wanted to know.

"Two of our cost areas are well under budget." I was thinking of the budget items that I had inflated to offset some production losses that I had anticipated because of the bad design. Phil didn't know about that.

"You mean if we accept their offer it would make us whole?"

"Yes," I said. "Head office would end up with the profit in our budget. I don't think they would let us litigate just to increase the profit – even supposing that a judge would allow it."

He was silent for a while. "No, I guess they wouldn't," he said finally. "It just makes me mad to back down from a perfectly legitimate claim. How, do you think, did they figure out at what level we might settle?"

"I don't know," I said, "but they're no dummies! I like their offer to keep us on the bid list, Phil," I added, "that could mean a lot to us in the future. Besides, they really appreciate the way we coped with the adverse circumstances and that we brought the project in on time!"

"Well, okay," he said. "Lets accept their offer and get on with it!"

5

Phil Hates a Supplier

Our crews were in the process of commissioning the pumps and controls of a large pumping station. Besides the concrete shell, the project consisted largely of mechanical and electrical equipment. The various pumps had to be tested for proper rotation and current draws, and each control had to be tested for its proper application.

One afternoon, the commissioning supervisor called the office. I was out of town for a few days, and the call was referred to Phil. The supervisor reported that three high voltage fuses of the main switchgear had just blown. The fuses were special and no spare ones were available locally. He requested new fuses to be flown in by overnight courier. Phil asked him what caused the fuses to blow.

"Not known at this time; we're still investigating," the supervisor told him. Phil then authorized an emergency purchase of three replacement fuses and three spare fuses.

Two days later, the supervisor phoned Phil again and reported that they had isolated the problem but blew all six fuses in the process. Phil was angry but authorized another emergency order to replace the six fuses.

The cause was the Bakelite contact-support of one of the motor starters that had overheated and carbonized. Since both the main switchgear and the motor control centers were supplied by the same supplier, Phil put a "stop payment" on the invoices for the replacement fuses.

When I got back to town, a detailed report of the incident was on my desk, and I asked the commissioning supervisor to meet me right away. He arrived later that day and brought along the piece of Bakelite that caused the problem. I asked him why this hadn't been isolated after the first three fuse blowouts.

"Our testing crew didn't isolate a control circuit and that gave us false readings," he admitted to me.

"Well, in any case, the various fuses down line should've been coordinated to protect the fuses up line," I said.

"This coordination was the responsibility of the supplier and wasn't done properly," he replied.

"Do we have their coordination report?" I enquired.

"Yes."

"And what does it show?"

"It shows proper coordination."

"How does the supplier explain that?"

"They're at a loss, Les," he said with a shrug.

"I don't like it," I said, "This is going to end up in one big argument because of the high cost of the fuses." He made no comment.

I didn't have long to wait for the argument to start. Shortly after paying the items on the next statement from the supplier, I had a call from the credit manager wanting to know why certain invoices (for these fuses) weren't paid. I told him that Phil had put a "stop payment" on them. I tried to explain to him that the reason for this action was their faulty equipment, which had caused the fuses to blow. He didn't have an answer and said that he would report this to his management.

The next day, I got a call from Henry Ralston, the supplier's local manager. Henry and I had had a few run-ins before – nothing serious.

"Can you set up a meeting with Phil?" he wanted to know.

"Sure; can I tell him what it's about?" I played dumb.

"It's about you people reneging on your purchase orders, that's what it is about!"

"I'll talk to him and get back to you, Henry," I said.

"You do that!" he said and hung up.

Phil wasn't too anxious to meet Henry. He told me to

handle it. I phoned Henry and told him, "Phil wants me to handle the problem."

"Won't do!" said Henry, "I need to talk to the big man himself!"

"I'll tell him and get back to you."

So, a meeting was set up for the following week. Phil and I had lunch that day, and he told me about a row he'd had with Henry when he was still involved in sales. "I'm looking forward to giving him back some of his own," he said.

Henry showed up at three o'clock with our salesman in tow. The first few minutes were spent exchanging pleasantries and talking about last night's game. Then Henry's face became serious. He told Phil that his company takes a dim view of purchase orders that weren't being honored.

"Cut the bullshit, Henry," Phil shot back. "You know damn well that the product you supplied us failed!"

"We don't deny that, but so did your testing crews. They should have caught the problem after the first fuse blowout!"

"That's your opinion! But if your fuse coordination had have been correct, even the first fuse blowout could've been prevented!"

"Phil, we can sit here arguing about whose fault it is all day," said Henry, "but that won't get us a solution."

"What do you have in mind?" asked Phil.

"I came here to propose to you that we split the replacement fuses' cost fifty-fifty," said Henry.

I had already told Phil over lunch that a fifty-fifty split would be a reasonable settlement. However, Phil pretended to be in thought for a while.

Henry finally said, "We're proposing this for the sake of our business relationship, not because we're admitting any fault."

That was the wrong thing to say to Phil. "Don't do me any favors!" he shot back. "You know damn well you've screwed up on this one!"

"If that's the way you feel about it, we have nothing more

to say to one another!" Henry was dead serious. "We'll pay for all the fuse replacements, but that's the last time you'll get a chance to do this to us. We won't sell you another screw!"

"Suits me fine!" Phil shot back, as Henry and the salesman left the office. I closed the door behind them and said to Phil, "I hope you realize that this supplier has quite a few exclusive products."

He laughed. "Sure," he said, "but we have the best purchasing connections right across North America."

Nevertheless, our purchases of these exclusive products proved very difficult in the next few months. Henry, too, had excellent connections right across North America. We had to do a lot of arm-twisting to convince the manufacturers to sell these products to us directly, but we did not get the supplier's favorite customer discounts.

I broached the subject with Phil one evening. "The best solution, Phil," I said, "would be for you to phone Henry and suggest to bury the hatchet."

"I wouldn't give that SOB that kind of satisfaction," he told me. "Don't forget, it was their equipment that caused all the problems!"

"Yes, but don't you agree that we're cutting off our nose to spite our face?"

"I don't care, Les. We need to teach them that our business continues without their favors."

A few months later, I found out that all these exclusive product shipments to us had received the nod from Henry with the proviso that he receives protection from the manufacturers by getting his regular commission.

6

Phil Trusts a Politician

Phil and I were relaxing over drinks at our favorite lounge. He had a grim look on his face. "What's eating you?" I said.

He was silent for another minute, and then said, "I think we have to issue a claim on the mining project."

I didn't respond. I was thinking, "What else is new?"

He said by way of explanation, "They screwed up our schedule. We have to perform our work, now, in unexpected dusty conditions."

"We knew from the outset that this is a dusty place," I said.

"Not to this extent," he replied grimly.

"What does Bill say?" I asked. Bill was reporting directly to Phil on this project.

"Bill doesn't know anything about claims," he said. "If we have any entitlement to a claim, you'll have to assess it, Les."

"I'm pretty busy at the moment, Phil, at least for another two weeks."

"That's okay. Make arrangement to fly out after you've cleaned your slate. The project has two months left in the schedule."

It took three weeks before I was ready to leave for a few days. After we landed, I rented a Jeep at the airport and checked in at a hotel near the mine site. When I arrived at our site office the next morning, I was shocked at the sight of our superintendent. He had sores all over his face and his hands.

"What happened to you?" I asked aghast.

"Some kind of corrosive in the dust," he replied sadly.

"Why don't you wear some protective clothing?"

"It's my own fault. I just don't always feel like putting it on

31

and taking it off for short periods inside. Our crews wear protection all day, of course. That's what slows them down!"

"Well, I'll have to go in and out a few times myself," I said. "You better let me have a mask, some gloves, and a pair of boots."

"No problem."

I spent till noon with him going over the details of our execution and the problems we've had – especially with the dusty conditions. Three things became evident to me: First, because of some labor problems with their mine workers, the owners had to cancel the time frame (window) they had given us to carry out our underground work in a dust-free environment. Second, all of the owners' equipment for the new plant arrived late, which pushed some of our work into the commissioning period and dusty conditions caused by equipment start-ups. Third, sixty percent of the new equipment had different operating characteristics from those specified, and this took extra work in the plant to make the required changes.

At noon, I was convinced that we had a solid claim for lost production, but I wanted to meet with John Castlegar, the owners' mining engineer, to find out if he had different ideas. He had agreed to give me an audience at 3 p.m.

"How's it going out there, Les?" he asked after I sat down in his office.

"I haven't actually had a good look around yet," I said, "but I understand that we're well into the commissioning phase. We still have a number of extras to complete – for changes to the operating characteristics of some equipment."

He nodded. "It's a bugger," he said.

"We're thinking of a claim for production losses on account of the dusty conditions, John," I ventured.

"Les, did Bill tell you that we were very generous in assessing your quotes for extra work?"

I shook my head.

"Yes, very generous, indeed! In fact, we think you were

more than compensated for any production losses on these extras!"

I stared at him for a while to try to detect any clues from his facial expression, but his demeanor was noncommittal. Finally, he thought of something else.

"You know, Les, I have prepared claims myself once, for two years – professionally, I mean, for one of the eastern claims experts."

"No, I didn't know," I said.

"Yes. That's what gave me my expertise to protect the owners from sharks like yourself."

"C'mon, John," I said a little hurt. "I'm only thinking of a legitimate claim for unforeseen conditions."

"I've told you already you've been compensated for that!"

"Yes, but you only mentioned extra work. What about the effects on our original work?"

"Most of your so-called 'original work' was carried out in clean conditions – and so was some of the extra work, by the way, although we allowed you a dust factor on all of it!"

"That still leaves us with a gap, John."

"Quit bullshitting, me, Les. The truth is that you guys underestimated this project. We could tell that from the tender prices."

"And who gets the benefit of our estimate shortages, John?"

"We do, I suppose, but don't ask us to compensate you for your mistakes!"

"I'm not asking that, John. Listen, I'm only asking you to consider a claim from us with an open mind!"

He looked at me for what seemed like an eternity. Finally, he nodded. "Okay, he said. "How long do you intend to stick around?"

"At least two more days – perhaps to the end of the week."

"Well, come and see me again before you leave. And bring an executive summary of your intended claim. I'll have a close look at it and let you know if I can support it."

"I'll try my best."

§

I phoned Phil from my hotel room and gave him a complete report. "I think John might support a claim," I finished.

"I don't trust the man," said Phil. "I've had a run-in with him a few years ago. He's tricky."

"Well, I'll give him the executive summary tomorrow afternoon and see where that takes us. I'll phone you again tomorrow evening."

"Okay."

The next day, I worked all morning and half the afternoon to put together as many facts and figures that I could lay my hands on. Sandy, our superintendent, helped me, of course. The final version of my four-page executive summary was ready at 4 p.m. John had agreed to see me at 4:30.

I sat across from him at his desk as he read the summary slowly. Finally, he looked up at me and said, "It has good detail, but I don't buy your quantification."

"What's wrong with it?"

"It smacks too much of a total-cost claim."

"I've made all the necessary adjustments for our mistakes, John; that makes it a *modified* total-cost claim."

"I don't even like *modified* total-cost claims, Les. They're too subjective, as far as I'm concerned."

"Well how else can the claim be quantified at this stage?"

He looked at me with some astonishment. "You don't expect me to help you with a claim against me, do you?"

"Why not?" I shot back with equal astonishment. "If the claim is legitimate, I don't see what's wrong with you giving me some advice. After all, didn't you tell me you have experience in claim preparations?"

He shook his head and looked at me for a long time. His eyes were speculative. "This conversation never took place," he said finally. "If you ever mention it, I'll deny it! But, if you want me to consider a claim, list all change orders, a brief description of the effect on your original work, and the work

34

hours of lost production."

I did a quick mental calculation. I would need an average of sixteen lost hours of production for each of 250 change orders to give me a claim of $300,000; with another $100,000 of change orders still to be approved, we could almost cover our shortfall. I nodded.

"One more thing," he said. "I want your claim submission before the project is finalized."

This only gave us one month to get it ready, and I would need the help of all project supervisors, who were extremely busy completing the work and commissioning the machinery. I nodded again, but I knew Phil would balk at the demand.

"Can I run a draft by you before I submit it officially?"

"For God's sake, Les! You want to get me fired?"

"Just a precaution, John."

"Oh, all right. I'll have a look at a couple of rows of your spreadsheet to see if you're on the right track. But I'm not promising anything! Understand?"

I phoned Phil again that evening. He didn't like the development. "I told you I don't trust John, and this proves my point," he said.

"What're you getting at?"

"Don't you see what he's trying to do? As soon as we give him a claim submission with this kind of break-down, he's got us by the short hair!"

"You'll have to explain that to me, Phil. I guess my mind's gone blank."

"Listen, Les. This kind of breakdown is usually the result of meticulous record keeping during construction. If you produce it after construction, your figures become suspect because they are too subjective. And John knows that. Once he has this evidence in his hands, you're at his mercy!"

In talking to John, I didn't detect an ulterior motive, but Phil had a point: If he did have such a motive, we were playing right into his hands.

"I don't see any other way out," I said. "If we prepare the claim our way, he'll reject it outright – he's as much as told me so – but if we prepare the claim his way, he may support it. Do you have another suggestion?"

"No, unfortunately not, but be careful! Get the supervisors to give you signed statements for the figures you use."

During the next three weeks, I prepared this giant spreadsheet. Since I had pressing obligations at our division office, I had to commute back and forth to the mine site for my interviews with the supervisors. The task of establishing an appropriate number of hours of lost production for each change order was a painstaking endeavor, but I finally managed to complete it on time. However, when I totaled the figures, I was short of my target, and I had to have another meeting with our supervisors to find out if they could support any upward adjustments. Nevertheless, the end result was $50,000 short of what I had hoped for, but I decided to run with it rather than lose the support of the supervisors. In any case, the outstanding change orders came to a higher amount than what I had estimated, which made Phil happy.

I went to see John and showed him the examples. He looked at them, nodded, and handed them back to me. He never uttered a word.

Another week later, I had the claim submission ready. Phil signed the usual letter of short explanation, with the hope for a speedy settlement, and we couriered the package to John's attention. A week later, I phoned John to find out if he'd received it okay.

"I received it, but you must understand that I'll have to go over it with a fine-toothed comb before I can formulate a recommendation for our board of directors."

"I understand, John."

A month went by, and no word yet from John. Phil was getting impatient and insisted that I give John another call.

When I got through to John, he said, "For God's sake, Les, don't be so impatient! I just finished studying your break-down, and our board of directors does not meet again until the first Tuesday of next month."

"Can you at least tell me what your reaction is to the claim break-down?"

"It looks okay as far as it goes," was all the answer I got out of him.

But Phil wasn't satisfied. He was stewing again and telling me at every opportunity that he didn't trust John.

One morning, Phil called me into his office and flatly told me, "I've made up my mind."

"You've made up your mind about what?"

"I know a politician in the mining district. We went to school together. I think I'll fly out to see him. I'm sure he can be of help."

I shook my head. "I think it would be wiser, Phil, if we wait till after the board meeting."

"That's where you're wrong, Les," he said gravely. "We would be playing right into John's hands. Once he convinces the board that our claim is invalid, it's going to be difficult to reverse their thinking."

There was nothing more I could say to talk him out of it. As he had said, "I've made up my mind!"

Two days later, Phil caught a flight to wine and dine his politician friend. He came back grinning. We had lunch together that day.

"It's in the bag, Les," said Phil, after we ordered our drinks. I gave him a questioning look.

"My politician friend will call the president of the mining company today and impress upon him to give us a favorable settlement."

I just shrugged my shoulders to indicate my doubt.

"I think my politician friend has a little more pull than your John, Les."

"I guess we won't have long to wait to find out, Phil."

John called me the next day.

"I'm rejecting your claim!" he said.

"What brought that on, John?"

"Ask your boss!" is all he would tell me.

Phil just laughed when I told him about John's phone call. "Sour grapes," is all he said.

A week later, we received an official letter from the president rejecting our claim.

7

Phil Stops a Walkout

I cleaned my desk to leave early one Friday afternoon; just then, Phil walked in.

"Getting ready to leave?"

"Yes. I have to pick up some supplies and sort through my tackle for a fishing trip tomorrow."

"Where're you heading?"

"Elk Lake."

"Trout?"

"No. Walleye."

"Gee, I haven't fished for walleye in over twenty years! Mind if I tag along?"

I looked at him dubiously. He didn't appear to be the outdoors' type. "No. Why don't you do that?"

"Who else is coming?" he wanted to know.

"Ed King, a retired friend of mine."

He nodded – after deciding Ed was safe company, I guess.

"We're leaving early," I said.

"That's okay."

"Well, then, I'll pick you up at six outside your apartment building."

"I'll be ready," he assured me.

When I drove up to his apartment building the next morning, I didn't recognize him at first. I had never seen him in any other attire than smart suits. This morning, he was wearing jeans, a khaki windbreaker, an old, gray hat with flies pinned to it, a checkered green shirt, and bluish-gray runners. Astonished, I asked, "Where did you get that outfit, Phil?" He

39

just smiled mysteriously. I introduced him to Ed, and we headed out of town.

"Does anyone want to stop for breakfast somewhere? No? Okay."

Two hours later, we launched our boat. I was deep in thought as we were trolling along the lakeside of the reeds when Phil said, "What're you thinking about?"

"Oh. I was just thinking about the best way to handle a problem on Monday."

"For heaven's sake, Les. Don't you ever get your mind off of work?"

"I'm trying to."

"What's the problem?"

"I had a call last night from our superintendent at the upgrader. There's been a walkout just before quitting time."

"What's the beef?" Phil wanted to know.

"Some infraction by a nonunion contractor earlier on Friday."

"Are nonunion contractors allowed on site?"

"Yes, but the owners have an agreement with the unions that nonunion contractors who come to the site must observe all union conditions."

"So, what're the owners doing about this infraction?"

"They have already done all they're going to do: They have issued an order to the nonunion contractor to cease the infraction and take immediate corrective actions. The contractor apologized and promised to do so."

"Then what's the problem?"

"The problem is, our workers claim that the company has a history of violating union conditions, and they want the company removed from site."

Phil thought about this while Ed was reeling in his first walleye. "Why didn't you mention this earlier, Les?"

"There's nothing we can do about it on the weekend, and I didn't want to spoil our fishing trip."

Phil just had a bite and tried to set the hook, but the line went slack on him. "Shit!" he said, then, "There is something we can do on the weekend."

"What's that?"

"Send a telegram to each of the unions, and tell them if they don't have their members back on site Monday morning we'll sue them for half a million dollars in damages."

"They'll just laugh at us."

"They won't laugh," said Ed. "Their international offices take a dim view of local unions that support illegal work stoppages."

"In any case, I don't think telegrams will reach the unions on the weekend," I said.

"They'll reach them," said Phil. "Send them to the business managers." Ed nodded his approval. He was an old union hand himself, and had been a union steward for many years.

"If I'm going to do this, I'd better do it now! There is a pay phone in the hotel across the lake."

"No need wasting good fishing time," said Phil. "Here, use my cell phone."

"I have my cell phone along, too, but cell phones don't work in this area."

"Mine does! It's one of those new gadgets that transmits via satellites." He handed me his phone.

I dialed for operator assistance and explained my mission. Thirty seconds later, I was talking to a telegraph operator. I dictated my message and, from my little address book, provided the names, and the business and residence phone numbers of the business managers. The reception was as clear as a bell. I was finished in less than fifteen minutes. "That's amazing," I said, as I handed the phone back to Phil. "I should get one of those, too."

"They're expensive as hell," said Phil. "I never thought I might put it to good use!"

We only caught three walleyes in the morning, and, being close to the hotel, Phil suggested that we stop for a cool glass

41

of beer and a snack. After lunch, I suggested that we try a sandbank I knew of a little further from shore. Our luck changed instantly, and by 4 p.m. we each had our limit. Phil was as happy as a lark. "Haven't had so much fun in years!" he exclaimed as we filleted the fish and put them in the icebox.

Early Monday morning, I had another call from our superintendent. "Everybody is back to work! What did you guys do on the weekend?"

"Oh, Phil has a special way of dealing with walkouts," I said.

The next morning, the superintendent phoned me again. "I think we're losing production, Les," he told me.

"Why?"

"Don't know. Nothing I'm able to pinpoint. Everybody appears to be working diligently, but we're not meeting our quota." He meant our estimated labor units.

"Keep a close watch on the situation, and phone me again tomorrow."

Over lunch with Phil, I mentioned our production loss at the upgrader. "I suppose it's a natural reaction of the workers," he said. "They resent being ordered back to work when they feel they have a legitimate beef. So, they're not putting out at maximum capacity for a while." I knew that was probably it, but his insight in human character never ceased to amaze me – probably his sales background, I thought. "It'll only last two or three days," he assured me, as I looked at him speculatively.

But by Friday, the situation hadn't changed. It got worse, if anything, according to the superintendent. "I'm heading out there on Monday," I told Phil. "I want to see for myself what's going on." He agreed with me.

However, as I had suspected, walking the site told me nothing. The evidence was in the figures, not in the discernable work pattern. So, I went to see the owners' labor-relations officer.

"We've got a problem, Jim," I said.

"What's your problem?"

"We've had a steady production loss last week."

"Any ideas?"

"Yes. We think there is a deliberate slow-down by our crews after the walkout."

"Hmm."

"We think the workers still resent your keeping the nonunion contractor on site. So, if they can't walk out, they'll just slow down."

"What do you want *me* to do about it, Les?"

"I don't know. Is there anything you can think of?"

"Well, there will be a damage claim if we break our contract with the nonunion contractor. So, that won't work. I could have a talk with the unions for you, Les."

I thought about this. He had an excellent relationship with the unions, but accusing their members of slowing down would not be well received by them.

"I don't know, Jim. You can't mention the slow-down." He nodded. "But perhaps you could explain to them your dilemma with the nonunion contractor. If they buy it, they'll get their members working again."

He nodded in agreement. "I'll do that, Les," he assured me. I felt better. It was a long shot, but it might just work.

I phoned Phil and told him about Jim's plan. "I like it," he said.

Two days later, I had a call from our superintendent. "I don't know what you guys did," he said, "but our production is going up again.

"Maybe the crews just had an off-week last week."

"No, Les, I don't think so."

A week later, he phoned me again. "Our production is back to normal," he said.

"Good."

43

"But some strange things are happening with the work of the nonunion contractor."

"Like what?"

"Oh, concrete in his pipelines – that sort of thing."

"Well, you better watch *our* work closely."

"You bet! We're doing that already, but we've had no problems so far."

"Well, keep it that way!"

I walked into Phil's office. He was busy reading *The Wall Street Journal*. "It seems our infamous nonunion contractor is experiencing some sabotage," I told him.

"Well, he's the one who caused the problem in the first place, isn't he?" He looked up at me with a smirk on his face. I just nodded and walked out.

8

Phil is in a Firing Mood

Mrs. Fitch, our conscientious bookkeeper, came into my office one morning in obvious distress. She was in charge of accounts payable and keeping the book entries of our purchases straight.

"Sit down, Mrs. Fitch. What's up?" I could see she was almost in tears.

"We have a problem with our hardware supplier." She gave me an anxious look. "A big problem!" she added.

"Tell me about it."

"Well, you'll remember I told you a few months ago that they were overbilling us on almost every invoice," she looked at me questioningly.

"Yes?"

"And we decided," she continued, "to pay them our purchase order amounts," she finished with the same look. I nodded.

"Well, here is what *they* did: For each overbilled invoice that we underpaid, they sent us a second invoice for the underpaid amount!"

I gave her an astonished look. "What did you do with that second invoice?" I wanted to know.

"I put it in a file folder and disregarded it!" she exclaimed.

I nodded my approval.

"The trouble is, these second invoices appear every month on their statement," she complained.

"Don't they ever correct their original invoices?" I asked her.

"Eventually they do, but it often takes several months."

I shook my head in disbelief. The foul-up was usually with phoned-in purchase orders, for which our purchasers used our negotiated prices and/or discounts, and the order taker used standard prices and/or discounts.

"But why all the distress?"

"Well," she said, "this morning I had a phone call from their credit manager, and he threatened to stop further deliveries of materials unless we pay these second invoices!"

"What!"

"Yes, Mr. Payne, that's what he told me!"

I shook my head again – in even more disbelief.

"Do you agree with me that these second invoices should *not* be paid?"

"I certainly do! It's bad enough that we're receiving so many overbilled original invoices. The second invoices are only making matters worse!"

"What should I do, then?" she wanted to know.

"Leave it to me. I'll phone him and set him straight!"

It was her turn to nod her head in approval. She left with a smile.

I finished a project I was working on and then put a call through to the supplier. "Mr. Kaminski, please." He answered on the second ring.

"Yes?"

"Mr. Kaminski?"

"Yes."

"Les Payne from Belvue Industrial Constructors."

"Oh, yes. What can I do for you?"

"For starters, don't threaten our bookkeeper! If you want to convey threats to us, phone me or Phil Potter." Silence. "For another thing, do you really expect us to overpay our purchase order amounts?" Our phoned-in purchase orders were usually mailed out within two or three days, and all prices would have been confirmed verbally during the phone call.

"I don't know what Mrs. Fitch has told you," he said, "but

our request for payment is justified."

"Like hell, it is!" I shot back. "I don't know at what school you were educated, but where I come from this borders on the ridiculous!"

"Listen to me," he said patiently, "your company started the wrong process in the first place when you made only partial payments on our invoices. Any time we receive a payment for an invoice, the invoice is dropped from our statement; that means, if we receive only a partial payment, we have to issue a second invoice to keep track of the difference. And if the partial payment is justified, we issue a credit invoice for the difference. And that means, the second invoice becomes payable. By the way, for your information, I have a degree in accounting."

"Fine. I still disagree with your math, but I'll think about it and get back to you."

Mrs. Fitch had heard me in the outer office and was beaming, but I felt sheepish. I usually don't get rude with people, even if I believe they talk nonsense.

I paced back and forth for a while, trying to clear my head. I was certainly dealing with an educated person in Kaminski, and, I asked myself, what if he is right? As soon as I asked myself this question, I felt like blinders had dropped from my eyes.

Immediately, I went into the outer office to see Mrs. Fitch and said, "Mrs. Fitch, I've thought about these second invoices. What do you do with the credit invoices when the supplier issues them?"

"Nothing needs to be done with them, Mr. Payne. The credits appear on their statement, of course, but they only reduce the statement amount, which we're paying. Nothing more than what should have happened in the first place – with the overbilled original invoice."

"That's just it, Mrs. Fitch. I believe the second invoices become payable as soon as credit invoices are issued for their overcharges. You cannot apply these credits without paying the second invoices. Otherwise, you're applying two credits!"

She looked at me in horrified disbelief.

"I'm going to phone Mr. Kaminski and apologize. Would you please get a check ready for him?"

She shook her head. "I don't believe this!" she raised her voice. "There is no way I can cope with this mess in my bookkeeping!"

"We'll figure that out later, Mrs. Fitch. Just get the check ready."

I walked back into my office and phoned Kaminski again. "Mr. Kaminski? Les Payne."

"What can I do for you?"

"First, let me apologize for my earlier rudeness."

"That's okay."

"Well, actually, it isn't! I was out of line to be offensive."

"Apology accepted."

"I gave the matter some thought, and I agree with you: The second invoices are payable when credits are issued. There'll be a check ready after lunch. Do you want to pick it up or should we mail it?"

"Mailing it will be fine."

"Thank you for your patience."

"Don't mention it."

Ten minutes later, Mrs. Fitch came into my office again. "Do you have the check ready?" I asked her.

"Yes, but I want you to know, I spoke to the accountant, Mr. Bushmeyer, and he agrees with me that the second invoices are not payable!" She meant the accountant who was assigned to us by our independent auditing firm.

"Fine," I said. "I don't have time to discuss it now. I'm just heading out for a meeting. Make sure the check gets mailed this afternoon."

I was late getting back to the office. Only Phil was still there.

"Had a busy day?" he wanted to know.

48

I nodded and sat down in his easy chair.

"Me too," he said. "Incidentally, I had a visit from our bookkeeper, Mrs. Fitch."

"Oh? What did she want?" Phil wasn't usually dealing with front-office people.

"She told me you've made a big mistake today, when you ordered her to pay some invoices she believes are not payable, and the accountant agrees with her."

"That's nice," I said sarcastically.

"Want to give me your side of it?"

"Sure. It's simple, really. We have some original invoices that were overbilled by our supplier. Mrs. Fitch is instructed to pay only our purchase order amounts for these invoices. When our supplier receives these payments, the original invoices get deleted from the statement, and second invoices are issued to keep track of the unpaid amounts. After the supplier investigates the underpayment validity, credit invoices are issued to adjust the original invoices. The credit invoices appear on the supplier's next statement. This effectively reduces the statement amount, and, consequently, our payment. However, the second invoices are still disregarded. In other words, we have taken a credit twice!"

Phil leaned back, taking sips from his coffee cup. After a minute, he said, "Makes sense. It's a typical example of the missing-dollar problem. Did I ever tell you the story of the boys who bought a bicycle together?"

I shook my head.

"Well, I heard this story a long time ago. It helped me a few times to identify solutions to accounting mistakes caused by mental blocks." He got my interest now. "There were three boys who longed to have a bike but couldn't afford one each, so they decided to pool their money and buy one together. They shopped around and saw one displayed in a bicycle shop for $45.00. The store owner had just gone for lunch and his son was minding the shop. The boys each paid the son $15.00, and off they went with the bike. When the store owner returned, he asked his son if he made any sales. The son told him that he'd sold the bike on display for $45.00, but the store owner was upset. He told his son that he had this bike advertised at $40.00 and forgot to change the tag. Since the son knew the boys, the store owner instructed him to take five dollars from the till and give it back to them.

"On his way to see the boys, the son decided that they would be happy receiving a dollar each, and he would keep two dollars for himself. He proceeded with this plan. That means, each of the boys paid only $14.00 for the bike, and three times $14.00 is $42.00, plus the two dollars that the son kept is $44.00, but they started out with $45.00. So, what happened to the missing dollar?"

I thought about it for a minute, and then laughed. "What missing dollar? You can't add the son's two dollars to the $42.00 again. It's already included in that amount!"

"Very good!" said Phil. "But you would be surprised to find out how many people don't get this answer. They usually can't get over the mental block that is created by the math logic of 42 plus 2 equals 44."

I nodded. We were both silent for a few minutes. Phil could be very pedantic at times.

"A mental block," he continued, "is usually supported by some sort of illogic which seems very logical to the person who has it. Often, you can't talk sense to people with mental blocks because they are convinced their logic is correct. They won't admit any other logic. You've heard the comic expression 'Don't confuse me with the facts, my mind's made up'?" I nodded. He went on, "And the only way a person can get rid of a mental block is by admitting another logic – just as you did when you said, 'Supposing he's right?'" He looked at me with a smile, and I was lost in thought for a moment.

"Give her a pink slip," said Phil finally.

I was so lost in thought that I didn't quite catch what he had said. "Sorry. What did you say?"

"Give Mrs. Fitch a pink slip."

"Why, Phil? She's conscientious and a very good worker!"

"That's not good enough for someone in her position. We can't afford mistakes in her work."

"I can try to explain this mistake to her."

"Yes, but you can't watch over her to catch every mistake that comes along. No, believe me, it's best to give her a pink slip."

"What about the accountant?" I wailed. "His mistake is even worse!"

"I agree. Firing him requires corporate approval. I'll take care of that." I looked at him for a long time. "It's best this way, Les," he assured me. "It has to be done!"

Mrs. Fitch just shook her head when she got her pink slip. She probably figured we were all nuts. But I don't know what happened to Mr. Bushmeyer. I never saw him again.

9

Phil Wants an Elevated Project

One morning, I came into the office at 7 a.m. in the hope to spend a quiet hour to concentrate on my monthly forecasts. Phil was already in his office reading *The Wall Street Journal*. He looked up and said, "You're early today."

"Yes. I want to finish my monthly forecasts."

"Sit down for a minute. I want to run something by you." I raised my eyebrows. "It's a different type of project," he said. I waited. "An elevated railway system." I raised my eyebrows again. "It's very simple construction, really, Les, but very costly. A real revenue booster!"

"Also high risk for us, Phil. Completely out of our league!"

"I don't think so. The project consists mainly of four components: the pre-cast concrete structure, of course, the train rails, the power pick-up rail, and a metal plate mounted between the train rails – a kind of stator, you know, like the housing of a motor, if you imagine the train to be the rotor of the motor. No moving parts, Les, except the train!"

"Surely, Phil, the train must have a motor or motors to drive it, and motors are moving parts."

"That's just it, Les! The train doesn't have any drive motors!"

"I don't get it."

"Well, do you remember your motor theory from school?"

"Yes?"

"You have two main parts to a motor: the stator – the outer housing – which is stationary, and the rotor, with the shaft, which rotates inside the stator." I nodded. "Okay. Now imagine flattening the stator to a straight piece of metal and

52

lengthening it – for miles if you will." I looked dubious. "The metal plate between the train rails I mentioned earlier?" I frowned and nodded. "Then imagine the train over top of this metal plate." I nodded again. "Mounted under the train, in close proximity to the metal plate, electromagnets that get their power from the pick-up rail." He looked at me questioningly to make sure I was following him. I gave him another nod to encourage him to go on. "That makes our train an effective rotor. And the train with the metal plate below it combine to make an effective motor!"

I closed my eyes for a minute to absorb this information. Of course! What a ridiculously simple invention!

"You're not an electrical engineer, Phil. How on earth did you grasp all of this?"

He laughed. "I read it in a magazine – a special article on the proposed elevated railway system. It's not a new idea, but it's being introduced here for the first time. That's when I decided to make an application to have us added to the list of bidders."

"That'll be quite an accomplishment, if you can pull it off. We have absolutely no experience in this type of construction. I imagine there is quite a bit of accuracy required to install the components – the train rails, the stator metal plate, the power pick-up rail, if you know what I mean – precision mechanical work, I dare say. We don't have mechanics that carry out this type of work, Phil."

"I thought of that. I think our millwrights could do it."

I nodded. "That's a possibility, Phil, but we may run into jurisdictional problems with our electricians. How're we going to resolve that?"

"There is nothing electrical about the metal plate."

"There is nothing electrical about fiber-optic cables either." I was referring to a dispute we had between our plumbers and electricians. The plumbers claimed fiber-optic cables because, traditionally, they installed glass products. The electricians claimed that light transmission is a form of electrical energy.

Phil knew that we always had these squabbles between trades.

"If we have to use electricians," he said, "the production will suffer. Millwrights are more adept at leveling equipment."

"Phil, you know that productivity is never part of the criteria in jurisdictional disputes."

"Yeah."

"So how would we prepare the estimate?"

"Assume the worst."

"We might as well not waste our time."

"The other bidders will have to do the same," he said.

"There's always someone who'll take a chance, Phil." He just shrugged his shoulders.

When Phil had his mind set on a course of action, trying to talk him out of it was like trying to move a mountain. So, three weeks later, when we received the tender plans and specs, I prepared the usual risk analysis for head office. Phil had a look at it before I couriered it and mumbled that these analyses were a waste of time – our lawyers had no conception of the realities involved. But it wasn't the lawyers who responded this time: Cliff himself gave me a call.

After the usual niceties, he said, "About this elevated railway project, Les."

"What about it?"

"How serious are you about it?"

"Phil wants us to try something new, Cliff. He thinks the simplicity of construction gives us a golden opportunity to break new ground and, at the same time, boost our revenue and profit significantly."

"But what do you think, Les?"

"It's in my risk analysis, Cliff." I learned the hard way not to expand on my risk analysis too much.

"I know. I know. Do you wish to add something?" A typical question of his that could get me into trouble no matter how I answered it.

"The main problem, as I see it, could come from jurisdictional hassles, as I have reported. Other than that, the metal plate between the train rails is not a standard product. I wouldn't know how to evaluate quotes we may receive for it. I don't even know who would supply it."

"We may be able to help with that. In any case, I'll ask Phil to come to head office to explain this venture to the board committee."

I knew Phil hated these meetings: If he convinced the board committee of the profitability of a venture, he invariably stuck his neck out, and if he didn't convince the committee, he wasted a lot of time and our precious marketing budget.

"You want me along, Cliff?"

"That's up to Phil."

Later, over a drink, Phil said, "Your damn risk analysis for the sky-train project has caused a stir at head office."

"What did you expect, Phil? We're charting unknown territory."

"Cliff wants me to meet with the board committee next week."

"It'll be a good change for you. You know what they say: A change is as good as a rest."

"Pah!" He was reflecting for a few moments. "Perhaps you should come along?"

"I'm sure you can handle this by yourself, Phil."

"You know more about these jurisdictional issues, if they come up."

"The board committee may be more interested in profit losses."

"Yes, but profit losses may be tied to jurisdictional problems, in this case."

"For what day is the meeting scheduled?"

"Wednesday."

"Bad day for me. I have to attend a site meeting at the upgrader."

"Get somebody else to attend for you."

That wouldn't even be necessary. I was just going to sit in to get the feel for what's going on. "Okay," I said. "When do we head out?"

"Tuesday evening. The meeting is set up for 9 a.m."

I hated these early-morning meetings. I was still fighting my jet lag at that time.

I would've preferred a hotel near head office, on the outskirts of town, but Phil picked a French-chain hotel downtown because, he said, he liked the food there. However, this meant getting up an hour earlier for a 45-minute cab ride. We arrived at head office with a half hour to spare – Phil believed in being early. The receptionist showed us into a small meeting room and brought us coffees. Phil read *The Wall Street Journal*, and I rescanned my risk analysis.

At 9:15, the receptionist poked her head into the room. "The committee is still busy with another project," she informed us, "but it won't be long now."

Phil just nodded. I started to get bored and searched a side table for an interesting magazine. No such luck. I went out and asked the receptionist for the local newspaper in the hope to find a crossword puzzle. She had already removed the puzzle for herself. When I got back into the meeting room, Phil tossed me a section of *The Wall Street Journal*. "Here, keep up with world affairs," he advised.

Phil started to look at his watch every five minutes but continued to study his "world affairs." I excused myself to go to the washroom. On the way back, I asked the receptionist how the committee is coming. She just shrugged. When I got back into the meeting room, Phil uttered his first curse. "Goddamn inconsiderate," he muttered. I opened one of the stale-dated magazines and found a half decent crossword puzzle in it.

At 10:15, the receptionist came into the room with an urn of hot coffee. "Sorry, gentlemen, but the committee is still tied up." Phil grunted. I smiled at her. "Thanks anyway for the coffee," I said.

An hour later, Cliff came rushing in. "I'm really sorry about the delay. Perhaps it would be best if you had an early lunch first. I've rescheduled the meeting for two o'clock."

We walked five blocks to a nearby hotel with a lounge. Phil ordered himself a double martini. I felt likewise, but decided on a beer. After downing a big swallow, Phil started again about the inconsiderate treatment we were getting. I told him, "Let's enjoy our lunch." Phil took this literal. We ordered steak sandwiches and never discussed the upcoming meeting.

This time, Phil didn't insist on being a half hour early, and we arrived at head office just before two. The receptionist immediately rushed us into the main boardroom – big enough for twenty people. Cliff and two other gentlemen were already waiting for us. He introduced them as two of the company's independent directors. Both were elderly. One, a Mr. Blackstone, was a ruddy-faced chap. I wondered if his complexion was the result of too much alcohol. The other, a Mr. Osborn, was sallow-faced and mean looking. I guessed both of their ages to be close to seventy.

Cliff opened the meeting by expressing his concern to the independent directors about our proposal to bid on an off-line project. Both elderly committee members nodded gravely. I had the feeling that Cliff was repeating himself for our benefit. Then, Cliff sat back and looked at his cohorts.

The two elderly gentlemen immediately addressed Phil. They bombarded him for a good thirty minutes with a dozen different ways to ask the same question: How can he be so certain to produce the forecast profit under such risky circumstances? Phil fielded their questions well for a while, but I detected a change in his voice, and his face had begun to flush.

Suddenly, they changed tack. "What is the possible benefit to the division and, more importantly, to the company to engage in such a risky venture?" Mr. Blackstone wanted to know. Phil relaxed. He seemed more comfortable answering this question. For the next ten minutes he spun an unconvincing yarn about developing experience in a new field of endeavor. The two elderly gentlemen looked at each other skeptically.

"Not much of this type of construction around," offered Mr. Osborn. Mr. Blackstone nodded in agreement. Phil tried a little harder to convince them. I had the feeling his effort was in vain. One of them finally asked Phil what market research he had conducted. "None, actually," he admitted, "but it stands to reason that many cities in North America are in dire need of sky trains." Both elderly gentlemen shook their heads sadly. Wrong answer, I suspected. "Cliff," said one of them, "we can't approve this project without a proper market research. Our board won't have it!" Cliff ignored the comment.

Mr. Blackstone turned to Phil again. "What about manpower?" he wanted to know.

Phil misunderstood. "We have no manpower shortage in our area," he assured the elderly gentleman.

"I mean, where're you going to get the specialized manpower for this project? It's not the type of work that comes along every day!"

Phil assured him that we could train the workers. Wrong answer again.

"Who's going to train the workers?" Mr. Osborn wanted to know.

Phil was squirming now. He looked at me for help, but I pretended to have missed the cue. "Perhaps we can search for trainers in cities with sky trains," he offered.

Both elderly gentlemen shook their heads sadly and looked meaningfully at Cliff, who ignored them again.

I was beginning to enjoy myself when Cliff turned to me and said, "What really concerns me, Les, is how you're going to get around the inevitable jurisdictional problems."

I turned red. I had mentioned the potential jurisdictional

problems in my risk analysis but had offered no solution. The two elderly gentlemen seemed to notice me for the first time since introductions. I think they were surprised that Cliff had asked me to offer an opinion. Both stared at me sternly.

"I don't know, Cliff," I said quietly. "It seems like a no-win situation regardless which way we push it."

Cliff nodded. "Did you investigate how the jurisdictional issues were resolved in other areas?"

Darn it! I should have thought of that before the meeting! "Not yet."

Cliff gave me a disapproving look; turning to his cohorts, he said, "I think we've pretty well covered it. Do you have any other questions?" Both elderly gentlemen shook their heads; turning to Phil, he said, "We'll let you know our decision next week."

Phil and I got up, shook hands with them, and left. We asked the receptionist to order us a taxi and headed straight for the airport.

Phil was silent for a while; then he turned to me and said, "What do you think?"

"About which way they'll decide?"

"Yes."

"I think they'll turn us down."

"I don't read it that way. It's a straightforward project – simple, good revenue, little risk. They would be stupid to turn down this golden opportunity!"

I nodded my I-hear-you nod. He was satisfied. On our return flight, fortified by two double martinis, he supported his opinion by pointing out some questions and remarks from the elderly gentlemen. I agreed with him on what was said, but I didn't mention that I had a different interpretation of the meaning.

It was the following Thursday when Phil received the answer in a memo from Cliff:

The committee wishes to thank you for bringing the sky-train project to its attention. However, since there is no shortage of the company's main-line work in your area, the committee recommends that you concentrate on that work for the time being. For future sky-train projects, the committee will conduct a more extensive market research and risk analysis. You will be informed of its outcome.

"Fools!" said Phil. "By the time they make up their minds, all of our opportunities will be gone!"

10

Phil Qualifies a Tender

We were in the last week of finishing an estimate for a big industrial plant when Deb, Phil's secretary, came to me with a message that Phil wanted to see me.

"Are your tender qualifications typed up yet?" he wanted to know.

"Yes, except for our separate prices."

"I want you to add a qualification." This should be interesting, I thought, because he has no inkling about this project.

"We had a contractors' meeting yesterday," he continued, "and everyone was in agreement that we should support the association's new contract form." I looked at him with expectation. "You know?" he explained, "Add a qualification in our tenders to the effect that our tenders are based on using the association's contract form."

"Not a good idea, in this case, Phil."

"Why not?"

"We're bidding to a good customer, whose contract form we've been using many times."

"Okay, but you know yourself that the industry has to do something about the proliferation of contract forms – mostly bad ones, I might add!"

I nodded. He was right, of course. "But why couldn't this be accomplished by an association lobby?"

"It was tried, Les, with little success."

"I'm not sure about this method, Phil. It'll sure piss off our customers. Besides, is it even legal?"

"Sure, it's legal! We can put any qualification we want in

our tender!"

"Yes, and our customers don't have to accept it!"

"What can they do if all contractors use the same qualification?"

"That's what I meant when I questioned the legality – the concerted effort of a bunch of contractors – ganging up on customers, you know?" I gave him a questioning look. "It smacks too much of collusion." He looked at me in astonishment. I don't think he had thought of that aspect.

I took advantage of his silence and said, "Have you looked at this from our customers' view point, Phil?"

"What are you getting at?"

"Well, suppose you were calling for tenders on a construction project. Wouldn't you want to specify the conditions under which it is bid?"

"Of course!"

"And the use of a specific contract form: Wouldn't that be one of your conditions?"

He looked at me again, a little deeper in thought now. "Don't try to confuse me with your misplaced fairness, Les. You know damn well that most of these individual contract forms contain unacceptable conditions that we can't fight single-handedly. We need an association to do that for us! In any case, I have committed myself, along with the other contractors, to stipulate this qualification in our tenders. Our vote was unanimous!"

I shook my head. "I'll put it in if you say so, Phil, but I have a bad feeling about it."

"When is this tender closing?" he wanted to know.

"Next Wednesday."

"Well, type the qualification in for now, so that we won't forget it. We'll discuss it again before submitting the tender."

As I came through the entrance to our main office on Monday morning, Deb met me with a worried look. "Phil's in the hospital," she said.

"What happened?"

"He slipped on the sidewalk to his apartment building and bumped his head."

"I better go and see him this morning. What hospital is he in?"

"University. But he's not allowed visitors until next weekend."

"Why not?"

"He's had a mild concussion, and his doctor ordered complete rest for five days. But I ordered flowers for him."

"Good girl!"

I poured myself a cup of coffee and went to my office to think things over: The tender closes on Wednesday. Normally, Phil would sign it. No problem. I had signing authority. But there was this damn tender qualification he had requested. I would have talked him out of it before tender closing. Could I just leave it off – forget about it? No, that wouldn't do. He would be upset. Darn it! If I could see him, I could discuss it. Well, it can't be helped now. I would just leave it in and hope for the best.

I didn't have long to wait for a reaction. Our customer's contract officer, a chap by the name of George Finning, called me at 11 a.m. on Thursday.

"Hi, George!" I said. "Did you call to tell me to mobilize a crew?" At that time, I didn't know where we stood with our tender.

"Like hell!" he shot back. "I called to tell you that we might have to reject your tender!"

A good sign! I thought. He probably wouldn't call unless we were low. And he was using the word "may."

"What's wrong?" I said, with as much surprise in my voice as I could muster.

"What's *wrong?* Don't play dumb with me, Les! You're too intelligent for that!"

"George, seriously, I think we submitted a perfectly valid tender to you."

"Not with your damn tender qualification about using an association contract form! You know damn well we can't accept that! Besides, what's wrong with our contract form? You've signed it a number of times without objections!"

"George, believe me. There's nothing wrong with your contract form. The problem is, Phil is not in the office this week, and he left prior instructions to add this tender qualification: some resolution of the association to promote a uniform contract form in the industry."

"Well for your information: You are less than one percent below the second bidder, another of your damn association members, and he has already told us he's withdrawing that same tender qualification. So, it's up to you to decide if you want to withdraw it also. I'm giving you till 2 p.m. to make up your mind. After that, we'll make our decision."

"I'll phone you before two, George."

"Good," he said and hung up.

What to do? I could phone Cliff, of course. I knew he wouldn't stand for any bullshit. But I didn't want to get Phil into any trouble. I decided to take my chief estimator for lunch to discuss the situation. Herman was as straight as a totem pole, and just as awesome.

"We've got a problem, Herman," I said, after we'd ordered our drinks. "Or, rather, I've got a problem, I should say, and I want your advice."

"Shoot."

I told him about Phil's tender qualification and my phone conversation with George Finning this morning.

"Phil's a fool – always has been when it comes to customer relations," was Herman's only reaction.

"That may be so, but what am I to do about this mess now? I'm damned if I do and I'm damned if I don't. I just don't want to act directly against Phil's instructions."

"What would Phil do if he were here?"

"I don't know. Probably withdraw the qualification. Cliff would bite his head off if he found out that we've lost a project on account of this nonsense."

"Well, there is your answer, isn't it?"

"I suppose so."

I phoned George immediately after we came back from lunch.

"I'm withdrawing the tender qualification, George."

"Smart boy," he said. "We'll process our contract with you next week. In the meantime, you can do some unofficial mobilizing to save time. Oh, and by the way," he added, "don't pull a stunt like that again on us!"

"Don't worry, George. And thanks!"

"Don't mention it, Les."

I phoned the hospital early Saturday morning to find out if Phil could receive visitors yet. Affirmative. So, I picked up the latest Robert Ludlum book I was sure he hadn't read yet and went to see him. He lay there looking glum, and paler than I remembered him. A cotton gauze pad was taped to the back of his head.

"What're you trying to do to yourself, Phil?"

"Icy patch on the sidewalk outside my apartment building. The caretaker hadn't sanded yet," he complained.

"You probably walked outside in your leather shoes."

"As a matter of fact, I had my overshoes on." He silently stared at the ceiling for a while. I waited patiently for him to say more. I didn't want to tire him with idle talk. Suddenly, he said, "How did the tender go?"

"Okay. We were low. George Finning is sending us a contract next week."

"You mean he's accepted our tender qualification for the association contract form?"

"No. We've had to withdraw that."

He gave me an accusing look.

65

"We were less than one percent below the next bidder, who had withdrawn the qualification before we did."

He looked astonished. "Who is the second bidder?" he wanted to know.

"Burkhart."

"The SOBs! They also voted in favor of the association's resolution!"

I shrugged. He looked at the ceiling again for a minute. "You did the right thing," he said finally. "Next time, we word the qualification differently. Next time, we'll say, a contract form, other than that of the association, shall be used only with our permission. That way, we're promoting the association's contract form, and we won't have to withdraw the qualification."

It was my turn to be astonished. Who said that Phil wasn't politically astute?

11

Phil Outsources the Payroll

One day late in February, I was gazing out the window of my office at a gentle snowfall when Trisha knocked at my open door. Trisha was our payroll clerk. She also did some secretarial work for me.

"Can I have a word with you, Mr. Payne?"

"Sure. Come in and sit down. What's on your mind?"

She began by telling me how overworked she was. This line always tells me that there's something wrong with the person rather than the job – she is, after all, working regular hours; the usual problem is a self-defeating attitude. After giving me a wide-eyed look, she wanted to know if I appreciated what she had to do to get out the weekly payroll – especially on days when I loaded her up with additional secretarial work.

"What it comes down to," she finished, "is that I want a raise!"

I gave her an appraising look. "You mean a raise would ease your workload?"

"It would make me feel better – more appreciated," she answered.

"Well, Trisha, you know our company policy: We give raise considerations in April, to become effective on the first of May, which is only two months away."

"That's not good enough, Mr. Payne. I want a raise now!"

"I can't make an exception for one person Trisha. There is the rest of the staff to consider."

"If I don't get a raise now . . ."

"Then what?"

"I'll have to give you two weeks' notice."

I looked at her speculatively. She was certainly *not* underpaid. Her salary was at the high end for her position. I was wondering if *she* fully appreciated the delicate position management is in when trying to keep a proper balance in the staff's pay scales.

"How much of a raise did you have in mind, Trisha?"

She gave me a dollar figure that was close to twenty percent of her present salary.

"I'll think about it for a day and let you know tomorrow," I told her.

"That's fine," she said and left my office. I could have given her an immediate decision, but she may have thought I hadn't considered it properly.

Truth be told, I had already given some thought in the past few weeks to the payroll-processing method we were using. Our method was still widely used, but it depended too much on manual labor. Every time we ran into sick days, vacations, or turnover of staff, we were facing critical disruptions. Outsourcing this function looked very attractive to me. I mentioned this to Phil when we were having lunch.

"Couldn't agree with you more," he said, "but head office is insisting on doing the payroll in-house."

I told him about Trisha's demand for a twenty percent raise.

"She's getting top wages now, isn't she?"

"Yes, but she thinks the raise would make her more appreciated."

"Is she threatening to quit if she doesn't get the raise?"

"Yes."

"So, what're you going to do?"

"I'll advertise for a replacement."

"You may not get someone with her payroll experience."

"I know. I'll contact our payroll system salesman. He'll probably know someone who'll work part-time until the new girl is trained."

"Good luck!"

"Thanks."

Next morning, I called Trisha into my office and said, "I've given your request some thought, Trisha. I think it is best if I advertise for a new position. You're welcome to apply, of course."

"Apply for my own job? You've got to be kidding!"

"No, no. It won't be exactly the same position. I'll put the emphasis on secretarial work. We'll update our payroll system. Payroll processing will take less time in the future. The ad will be in the paper tomorrow. By the way, your offer to stay two more weeks is appreciated."

"I don't think I'll apply, Mr. Payne."

"That's up to you, Trisha. But all things being equal, I would give you my preference. Besides, it would be the only way I could consider giving you a raise at this time."

She gave me a dubious look as she left my office.

By the following Monday, I had received more than twenty applications for the position. I short-listed five women and interviewed them on Tuesday. Trisha was not one of them. She had overpriced herself. The one I settled on had some payroll knowledge, good secretarial experience, and wanted less pay than Trisha was getting. However, she was not available until the first of April. The next day, I called our payroll system salesman.

"Brent? Les. How are you?"

"Fine. Haven't heard from you in awhile."

"I've been pretty busy."

"Yeah, haven't we all. What can I do for you?"

"I have a little problem. Trisha is leaving us, and her replacement is not available until the first of April. Would you know somebody who can process our payroll on a part-time basis?"

"Might be. Yeah, I know a woman who might do it. I'll

have to phone her to find out."

"I would appreciate that, Brent. Let me know as soon as possible."

"If she's available, I'll get her to phone you directly, Les."

"Suits me. Thanks, Brent."

"Don't mention it."

My private phone line rang right at 5 p.m., after everyone had left the office. I picked up the receiver. "Hello?"

"Mr. Payne?"

"Yes."

"My name is Mary Bowker. Brent Arkin asked me to call you."

"Oh, yes. You're the part-time payroll clerk?"

"Well, I'm actually working full-time right now. But I'm willing to put in extra time for a couple evenings a week."

"I'm afraid two evenings a week may not be enough, Ms. Bowker. Presently, the work is taking four days a week."

"I'm very familiar with your system, Mr. Payne. I'm doing a payroll for more than 400 employees in less than two days. Remember, I won't have the daily disruptions in the evening. So, I'm sure I can do your payroll in two evenings if the time sheets are filled in properly."

"What do you mean by 'filled in properly'?"

"I mean hours totaled properly, wage rates and special deductions entered, and so on."

"No problem. We'll see to that."

"I'm not cheap, Mr. Payne."

"What're you charging?"

"Twenty bucks an hour, including benefits."

"I think we can afford that." By my calculation, her weekly charge would be less than what we were paying Trisha for the four days she worked on the payroll each week.

"One more thing."

"Yes?"

"You're not right down town. I want to be picked up from

down town and brought back again each evening."

I supposed that one of our late-working estimators could manage this. "Okay. Anything else?"

"When do you want this work done?"

"How about starting in the week after next, say Tuesday and Wednesday evenings?"

"Fine with me."

We made out the time and place and hung up.

On Trisha's last day, she came into my office to say goodbye. "It's been nice working with you, Mr. Payne. Too bad things didn't work out. I wish I could have stayed another two weeks until the new girl starts, but I'm starting my new job next week." She had tears in her eyes.

"It's been nice working with you, too, Trisha. I hope your new employer pays you the salary you wanted."

"In fact, I'm starting at a lower salary than what I'm making now – at least for the three-month probation period, you know?"

"Well, I'm sure they'll recognize your value pretty soon."

"I hope so!"

"Good luck! And keep in touch Trisha."

"Thanks. I will, Mr. Payne."

That evening, Phil and I were relaxing over drinks in our favorite lounge – Phil with his double martini and I with my Chablis.

"Trisha is starting in a new job next week – at a salary lower than we were paying her."

"Doesn't surprise me," said Phil. "Some employees don't know when they're well off."

"I think she regretted leaving us."

Phil shrugged. "Let's forget about her. I have some good news for you. I've been able to convince head office to let us outsource the payroll."

"That's great, Phil! How did you manage that? I thought

71

they were insistent on handling the payroll in-house."

"I asked them why this is important to them. They said it facilitates their cost accounting and general-ledger entries. But they had already done some research themselves, and our bank told them that the bank can provide a cost accounting breakdown as well as electronic feeders into our general accounting system."

"Sounds like that removes head office's obstacles."

"It does, but they're still proceeding cautiously. Ours will be the only division to get the green light for now. They want us to settle things with the bank so that we'll be on stream by May first."

"That's excellent, Phil. I'll take care of that."

"Good. We'll not only save on overhead, but your concern about missing a payroll is also alleviated."

"I know! Gosh, You've sure made my day! – *And* my weekend, I should add."

He answered my admiring look with his Cheshire-cat grin. "Drink up! I'll order us another round."

12

Phil Hates Bid Peddling

We had closed a tender for a major industrial project a week earlier, and I received a letter from the prime consultant inviting us to attend a pre-contract-award meeting to discuss the scope of work and some commercial aspects. The meeting had been set up for Thursday at 1:00 p.m., the day before Good Friday, at the prime consultant's office located in a small city on the west coast.

I called my chief estimator, Herman Myers, on the intercom. "Herman, prepare yourself to fly out to the coast to attend a pre-award meeting with Burnside Engineering. They want to discuss our tender qualifications and the scope of work in general."

"Are we low?"

"They didn't say, but we must be short-listed."

"When's the meeting?"

"Next Thursday."

"Count me out, Les; I have planned a trip out of town for the long weekend."

"I'm sorry, Herman, but I can't handle this by myself. Most of the issues up for discussion will be technical and involving the estimate. Your presence is essential!"

"If I can rearrange my schedule, I want Easter Monday off."

"That's okay."

"Well, I better get busy and organize my papers for the meeting – make some notes as well."

"Good idea. I'll get Deb to make the travel arrangements. We'll probably book ourselves in at the Hyatt. It's the closest hotel to Burnside's offices."

"You don't intend to stay overnight?"

"No, no. We just need a room to freshen up and prepare ourselves – make some phone calls, and so on."

"Oh, I see."

I talked to Phil about the trip.

"Watch those cowboys," he said. "They're a mean bunch!"

"How do you mean?"

"I've had a bad experience with them a few years ago. In one of the tenders I was involved, we had a number of exclusions and qualifications. As each of these was discussed, they intimated that if we insisted on leaving them in place, we would risk losing the contract. So, we ended up withdrawing most of them, at considerable additional cost to us, as you can imagine! At the end, they asked us if we could suggest any alternatives, since our price is a little high." He looked at me with an ironic grin – signaling some devious practice.

"Did you give them any alternatives?"

"They knew more alternatives than we did, Les. This was just a ploy to get us to drop our price by a few percent."

"Did you test that, Phil?"

"We sure did! We gave them an alternative at actual savings, and they told us we were still considerably high. Later, I found out they pulled the same stunt on all short-listed bidders. The low bidder really fell hard for it!"

"What did he do?"

"He dropped his tender by five percent for an insignificant alternative – when he had been five percent low to start with! God, I hate bid peddling, and that's all it amounts to!"

"When was this, Phil?"

"About ten years back."

"Maybe things have changed since then."

"Maybe, but I doubt it."

"I might have to phone you if I get some strange requests."

"Phone me on my cell phone. I'll be leaving early for the

long weekend."

"You're lucky! I'm not even sure I'll be back in time to enjoy any kind of weekend."

"Well, good luck to you!"

"Thanks. It sounds like I'll need it!"

During the flight to the coast, I made myself some reminder notes on all the commercial aspects of the tender. Herman reread the specs. Our flight arrived early. We took the shuttle bus to the Hyatt and rented a meeting room. Then we went for an early lunch.

The meeting with the engineers was scheduled for one o'clock. We arrived at ten to one. However, in my experience, one-o'clock meetings seldom start on time, and this one was no exception. The engineering staff drifted in steadily from the lunch break till twenty minutes past one, and our meeting finally got started at 1:30 p.m. We were facing a panel of seven engineers representing different disciplines. After introductions, the chief engineer explained to us that we were short-listed for the project, and their task was to make sure that our tender complied with the specified scope of work.

Following this explanation, the panel members literally went over every clause in the specifications, starting with the General Conditions. Were we aware of this? Did we make provisions for that? Did our tender include such and such? One of the engineers acted as secretary and recorded our answers verbatim. It took almost two hours to go over the specifications. Then the chief engineer took our tender form from his file and went over our tender qualifications. By this time, I had the feeling that we were their chosen contractor, providing our tender qualifications didn't foul things up.

Their questions regarding these qualifications were almost accusatory, and one by one we agreed to remove most of the exclusions. I knew Phil wouldn't like it. He never minded us cutting costs, but cutting his profit was always a no-no. And removing our tender qualifications was tantamount to cutting profit.

Finally, the chief engineer said, "We're satisfied that your tender covers the complete scope of work now." He looked around at his fellow engineers and got nods. "There is only one problem." He looked at me.

"What's that?" I wanted to know anxiously.

"Your tender price is over our budget." This was nothing new. Engineers are notorious for establishing low budgets – either to appease the owners or to keep contractors' prices in line or because they didn't know better. But Phil's words of caution came to mind.

"How much?" I wanted to know.

"Five percent," he said without hesitation.

I looked at him with some astonishment. Five percent was a lot when you had to meet strict specifications. Our estimated profit, or what was left of it after this meeting, wouldn't even cover that.

"We're not asking you to `lower your price," he continued. "Perhaps you could suggest some alternatives acceptable to us. I'm sure that would bring you in line with our budget."

I gave him a speculative look. Many contractors, given this opportunity, would offer some inconsequential alternatives at a five percent saving, just to land the job. Was he playing this kind of game? After all, they had already turned down alternatives proposed by us in our tender, which could have resulted in substantial savings to them.

"Think about it," he added. "Where can we reach you between six and seven this evening?"

"We have a room at the Hyatt," I offered.

"Okay, we'll be in touch to get your answer."

We said our good-byes and left. In the lobby, I saw the representatives of another contractor. I nodded to them. It was their turn now.

On the way back to the hotel, Herman asked, "Do you mind if I leave you and head back?"

"Don't you want to help me work out some savings?"

"I worked out some savings, Les – the ones we suggested in our tender. They turned them down, remember?"

"Okay, get going and have a nice weekend. I'll call Phil and find out what he wants to do."

When I called the office, Phil had already left. I made a note of my messages and called Phil on his cell phone. I gave him a quick overview of the afternoon's meeting. "What do you think we should do?" I asked.

"Nothing," he said. "I know their game. They'll turn down any consequential change proposals. All they're looking for is big savings for little or no change. And I'm not inclined to let them have our remaining profit." He stopped for a moment. "Give the hotel the forwarding number of our message center and check every now and then for messages. If they phone, we know we're either low, or the low bidder didn't fall for their tricks. Then we'll decide what to do next. If they don't phone, we know that the low bidder fell for their ploy and we're out of it. Now pack your things and fly home. Don't waste any more time on this. Enjoy the weekend!"

"You, too!"

They never phoned, and I was glad I took Phil's advice. A week later, we received a letter from them, thanking us for our attention and advising us that the contract was awarded to another bidder; also, expressing their hope to be dealing with us in the future.

Phil gave me an ironic smile. "I hope you've learned a lesson, Les."

Three months later, I had an opportunity to find out that the low bidder had indeed dropped his price by another five percent.

13

Phil Likes a Claim

Construction claims for disruptions, delays, and production losses are difficult to prepare and to prove at the best of times, and the best of times are when they are foreseen and prepared from the outset of construction.

We had such a claim on one major project where the owner had decided to carry out construction with multiple contractors and to supply all major materials. Phil immediately sensed that we were heading for disaster, and he issued instructions even before we had arrived on site to prepare for a claim.

Sure enough, his anticipation proved valid soon after we started construction. Some of the owner's materials were faulty, and various contractors took turns delaying each other. We had top-notch supervisors on site that knew how to prepare claims for these disruptions, but Phil himself was overseeing the process. He was clearly in his element. He called weekly meetings with the supervisors and, in addition to the usual documentation such as diaries, weekly field-progress reports, and authenticated pictures, he made sure that the required notices were served, that as-built schedules were maintained, and that accurate production measurements were established.

The owner's supervisory staff was quite aware of our preparations for a claim. In fact, they enjoyed following the process – probably learning from it themselves. They were sympathetic to our complaints and even co-signed our weekly field-progress reports, which detailed our constraints.

Slowly but surely, our claim-document file grew in a

systematic, organized fashion. Phil was very pleased. He made this claim his favorite topic of conversation. Every time we had lunch together, he was speculating on different aspects of the claim and how it would affect our bottom line.

"If claims are handled right, Les," he would remind me every time, "they can assure you of your budgeted profit." Meaning: Watch me how I handle them. I, on the other hand, encouraged him in his endeavor, as one would encourage a schoolboy to improve his grades. Phil appreciated that and became a little pedantic.

"One of the main things to remember with a claim," he would say, "is that you don't antagonize the owner – especially the owner's site staff. This site staff can be of great help by giving favorable reviews."

"We have a very good relationship with the owner's staff, Phil."

"Good! Keep it that way! Wine and dine them if you have to, and make sure they understand our side of things. Explain it in minutest detail."

"Yes, Phil."

On other days, Phil could be moody. "I know we have a good claim – ironclad, Les – but I almost think it's too good."

"What're you getting at, Phil?"

"Haven't you ever been suspicious of something that just seemed too good to be real?"

"Sure."

"Well, that's how I feel sometimes about this claim."

"Don't worry, Phil. I can't think of anything to do to improve it."

"Hearing you say that makes me feel better." He was happy again for a while. He knew I had prepared many claims myself, and I was keeping a close watch on this one as well.

Next time, he would become suspicious of our supervisors. This suspicion plagued him as long as I knew him. In his opinion, supervisors caused most of what went wrong on projects.

"Are you making sure our supervisors are careful to separate these claim causes from any other production-loss causes, Les?"

"You mean causes attributable to our own mistakes?"

"That's exactly what I mean – ours and our suppliers' mistakes."

"Yes, I am."

"Good. What about mitigations? We can't just assume that the owner will pay us for production losses unless we tried to mitigate them, can we?"

"No, we can't. And we're doing all we can to mitigate them."

"Good. I just don't trust these supervisors, Les. They don't have the same appreciation for the important claim issues as you and I have. Their minds are on getting the job done."

"I think these guys appreciate what is at stake, Phil; they've been through the hoop a few times before."

"Well, just make sure you keep an eye on them."

I nodded my assent.

Towards the end of construction, Phil wanted to know, "What are you telling head office about this claim?"

"Not much, Phil. So far, it's just a footnote to my monthly forecasts, and nobody has asked me any questions yet."

"That, too, makes me suspicious, Les. Maybe they think the risk is minimal."

I shrugged. In my experience with head office, no risk was ever "minimal." I remember one time when one of our projects was delayed for a couple of weeks at start-up. I thought it was a minor issue, but Cliff jumped on me with both feet: "How can you minimize the risk of this, Les?" he wanted to know. "The owners can hold this delay against you throughout construction; they may even oppose a legitimate claim you might have on account of it!"

Cliff was as claim-shy as anyone I've ever met. So, why was he silent on our present claim?

It only took us a week to finalize our claim submission at the end of construction, but Phil took another two days to blue-pencil it with minor changes he thought would make it more effective. After his changes were made, I delivered the submission to the owner's supervisory staff. They promised to let me know before passing it on if they had any objections. A week later, I received a phone call from one of them to tell me that everything looked okay, and they have passed it on with favorable comments from them.

Phil and I had lunch together that day, and I told him the good news. "Doesn't surprise me," he said. "I have never seen a better documented claim." And he ordered another round of drinks for us to celebrate the occasion. I've seldom seen him happier.

"What will be your next project?" I wanted to know – not altogether without self-interest, for his preoccupation with the claim kept him almost at arm's length from us.

"I think I'm ready to take some time off – ten days or two weeks, perhaps."

"Are you thinking of going anywhere?"

"Perhaps. I might take a cruise to Alaska. Right time of year for it."

"That would be nice. I always wanted to do that myself one day."

"You should. I hear it's one of the few places in North America with clean air!"

"When are you thinking of leaving?"

"As soon as I can finalize the arrangements."

A few days later, I had a call from Cliff. "How's it going, Les?"

"Fine. I'm rather busy right now. We've just wound down one project, and we're already starting another."

"Don't complain. Some of our divisions have a work shortage."

"Oh, I'm not complaining. What's on your mind?"

"I'm calling about your claim against Stanwick." Gosh! How did he get a hold of that one so fast?

"Yes?" I offered.

"It comes at an inopportune time, Les. Three of our divisions have major projects underway with Stanwick, and one division is in the process of negotiating another project with them."

"The claim is legitimate, Cliff. It even has the backing of Stanwick's supervisory staff."

"That only means something if we get serious with the claim."

"What are you trying to tell me?"

"Withdraw the claim, Les. It's best for our business relations with Stanwick at the moment."

"Phil won't like it, Cliff. He depends on this claim to bring in his budgeted profit."

"I'll talk with Phil."

"Is this your final decision, then – you're really serious about dropping the claim?"

"I am, Les. I'll make it up to you somehow."

"Okay, Cliff."

I wasted no time telling Phil about Cliff's request. I expected him to start cursing, but he stayed calm.

"Could be an advantage to us," he said.

"Would you mind explaining that to me? I'm a little dense today."

"We'll send head office an invoice for the claim, Les. Inter-departmental charges, you know?"

"That works only for services rendered, Phil."

"We *are* rendering a service, Les. Aren't we?"

"I guess so. But head office is not a profit center. They have no budget for this invoice."

"That's their problem. They can apportion it to the profit centers that benefit by this. Just send them the invoice before you withdraw the claim. See what happens."

"I'll do that."

Ten days later, I still hadn't heard any screams from head office, and I decided it was time to withdraw the claim. I can still picture the surprise on the faces of Stanwick's supervisory staff. "You'll never have a better one!" they assured me.

14

Phil Prepares a Five-Year Budget

Phil was often preoccupied with the division's yearly budget. I saw him many times stooped over a single sheet of paper on his desk: the latest monthly update comparing the accumulated income, expenses, and earned profit to the budget. In these moments, he was oblivious to the activity around him.

Occasionally, I asked him, "How are we doing, Phil?" and he would look up and give me a glassy stare. I took the cue and left him alone again. But away from his budget sheet, usually over lunch, I would repeat the question. He never gave me a happy answer. I gathered from his spare responses that his beloved profit was constantly in jeopardy.

The worst month was February, when we prepaid many expenses for the year, which used up a disproportionate budget amount. Phil would spend a long time with his calculator reapportioning the expenses. "I think we're okay," he would tell me over lunch. "God, I hate these budgets!"

One day, a memo from Cliff Jensen came addressed to "All Division Heads" with copies to their seconds-in-command:
"Please prepare a five-year budget for the Midwest division and submit it to head office no later than one month prior to the fiscal year-end."
Phil was livid: "What do they think we are, omniscient?" But he didn't dare to oppose Cliff openly. So, the two of us had a strategy meeting to plan the accomplishment of this seemingly impossible task.

We soon determined that our potential expenses would

have to be detailed, as was the case with our yearly budgets. We decided to use two adjustments each year: one for inflation and one for growth. Phil offered to look after the first if I look after the second.

"And how am I supposed to establish growth, Phil?" We both looked puzzled.

"Let's call it a day and discuss this problem over a drink," he suggested.

"Fine." A drink was always a big problem solver for us. But it took two drinks before we got back into the subject.

"What determines our growth?" Phil wanted to know.

"I suppose our desire and ability to grow."

"Yes, but also our opportunities. No amount of desire and ability can make us grow without opportunities!"

I had to agree with him.

"So, Les, let's find out what our potential opportunities are in the next five years. Let's phone our customers and engineering companies and ask them what they are planning for the next five years. Then we'll decide what percentage of that construction volume we're likely to get."

Of course, his "we" turned out to be me. I had to do all the phoning and gathering of information. The result was overwhelming. After only one week, I had a list of projects that added up to many billions of dollars. I asked Phil if he wanted more.

"No, I think that'll do for now. Let's work out some probabilities." But he had a preconceived idea that we should end up with at least ten percent of the available construction volume. Using that percentage, our final growth figure was absolutely staggering!

"Well, back to the drawing board," I suggested.

"Why? I think this volume is attainable, Les."

I couldn't believe my ears. "Even if it is, Phil, head office would never permit it."

"Let's find out."

A few days later, I had a call from Cliff. "Are you coming

to head office next week to discuss your risk analysis for the new PetroHi-G upgrader, Les?"

"Yes, I am."

"Did you help Phil with the five-year budget?"

"Yes, I did."

"I've never seen anything so ridiculous in my life! You guys must have some screws loose upstairs."

"Are you referring to the budget's aggressive growth pattern?"

"The budget's *megalomaniac* growth pattern, you mean!"

"Phil is just trying to draw our opportunities out here to your attention, Cliff."

"Well, he got my attention, all right! Are both of you coming next week?"

"Yes."

"Tell Phil we're setting time aside to discuss his five-year budget."

"Wouldn't it be better coming from you?"

"Just tell him, Les. See you next week."

"Okay, Cliff."

I went to Phil's office and said, "Head office is setting time aside at our meeting next week to discuss your five-year budget, Phil."

He just laughed. "Looking forward to it."

We arrived at Phil's favorite downtown hotel before six o'clock on the evening before our meeting and had our supper at Phil's favorite restaurant. I didn't bring up the subject of our next day's meeting until we had ordered our ports.

"I don't expect too much opposition to my risk analysis, Phil, but your five-year budget is another matter."

"What do you think they'll object to?"

"The aggressive growth pattern."

"Why do you think they'll object to that?"

"We've discussed this before, Phil."

"No, please, tell me. It might give me an idea how to

respond."

"Well, for one thing, we would have to hire more staff *before* we have the revenue to pay for it – assuming we'll ever get the revenue. That'll be their biggest objection, I think."

"I don't think they are stupid enough to object to *that*, Les. Every business before start-up has to spend money on overhead for expected revenue; the same applies to expanding businesses."

He was right. "All right, but they might want to know where we expect to get the staff for this rapid expansion."

"People will go to where the work is available, Les."

He was right, again. "Well, maybe the company has financial limitations," I offered lamely.

"Pah."

"No, I suppose not."

"I don't believe they'll have any good arguments against this budget, Les. For what time tomorrow is the meeting scheduled?"

"Ten o'clock."

"Good. We'll have time for a half-hour walk in the morning – clear our heads."

We arrived at head office with ten minutes to spare. The receptionist led us into the big boardroom.

"Coffees, gentlemen?"

"Yes, please."

We were the first to arrive. Right at ten o'clock, Cliff led two other committee members into the room. We knew Mr. Osborn, the sallow-faced, mean-looking chap, and Cliff introduced the new member as Harry Linquist, another independent director and retired lawyer. I liked him immediately. He looked like an outdoors' type: brown complexion, strong features, and slightly gray, black hair with white sideburns.

"Call me Harry," he said, as he shook our hands.

After everyone had settled down with a cup of coffee and exchanged a few meaningless comments, Cliff got down to business.

"Let's have a look at your risk analysis for the PetroHi-G upgrader, Les."

I opened my file and looked at him expectantly.

"Our main concern is the manpower situation. The project is going to be built in an area that has manpower shortages. You have identified this risk, Les. Tell us how this problem will be resolved."

"The unions will draw on manpower from neighboring states."

"Won't that affect the production adversely?" Mr. Osborn wanted to know.

"It will to some extent, but our supervisors know how to cope with that."

"What do you mean by 'cope' – live with it or improve it?" Mr. Osborn insisted.

"Our supervisors have experience with crews from different localities and know how to maximize the productivity."

Cliff asked a few more questions about the duration of manpower loading during construction; he had a quick look at his committee members and got an almost imperceptible nod; he turned to me: "You have our approval, Les." I nodded.

He turned to Phil: "Now, regarding your five-year budget."

Phil had lost last night's comfortable look.

"By the way, Phil," said Mr. Linquist, "do you intend to retire in the next five years?"

Phil was taken aback. "I haven't given it any thought," he said, "but I have no intentions at present to do so."

"Good! Because if those were your intentions, we would be wasting our time."

"The committee wouldn't want to saddle a successor of yours with an impossible task," Cliff explained.

Mr. Osborn cleared his throat. "We intend to approve your budget, Phil, but we're going to insist that you live by it!

We're not going to allow you to spend a lot of money on additional overhead without insisting that you produce the revenue to pay for it!"

"Perhaps you would like to think it over for a week and make some adjustments," suggested Mr. Linquist.

Phil was about to say something when Cliff cut him off. "That's an excellent idea, I think." He looked at his cohorts and got another nod from them. "It's settled then. You will have a second look at your budget and advise us in one week of any adjustments, Phil. Thanks for coming to meet with us, gentlemen." We were summarily dismissed.

Phil was silent until we were at the airport, got our boarding passes, and settled down in the lounge.

"Congratulations, Phil!" I offered.

He gave me a glum look.

"Well, you've got what you wanted, didn't you?"

"Don't tease me, Les. You know I never believed that they would approve this crazy budget."

"You still have a chance to make adjustments, Phil."

But I couldn't get him out of his glum mood. I suspected that he was torn between his ambition and his cautious nature. The board members told him they would hold him to his budget – what if he couldn't deliver?

For the next five days, Phil was unusually reticent. Then, during the morning of the sixth day, he called me into his office. "I want your honest opinion, Les. What, if any, adjustments should be made to this damn five-year budget? After all, you'll have to produce the revenue for it!"

"If it were up to me, Phil, I would budget for a twenty-five percent growth each year. I think that's attainable, and it will triple our revenue in five years. And if we end up with more, nobody is going to complain."

"It may *be* up to you, Les, before five years are up!" He looked for a while at his budget spreadsheet. "Okay," he said

89

finally, "I'll take your advice and make the adjustment."

On my way out, I heard him call Deb, his secretary, on the intercom: "Deb, we'll have to retype this damn five-year budget." She rolled her eyes as I walked past her desk.

In the afternoon, Phil was in a much happier mood. "Got time for a drink tonight, Les?"

"Sure."

Later, over our drinks, he said, "It's best this way, Les!" As if I had to be convinced.

15

Phil Refuses to Supply Replacements

Phil and I were going over our project list to determine how to improve our division's profit for the year-end. Head office had some strict rules about profit taking: unless a claim was pending, head office allowed half the budgeted profit to be taken after a project was certified to be 50% complete and the other half after the project was certified to be 100% complete. One time, when Phil tried to take a profit after 50% of a project was billed, Cliff reminded him that "billed" is not the same as "complete," even if the owners okayed the billing; "complete" for the purpose of our profit-taking policy means "erected" or "installed" – make no mistake about this!

Phil pointed his finger at one project that had been completely billed, but had no check mark to indicate its acceptance by the owners. "Why hasn't this project been accepted?" he wanted to know.

"The prime consultant has rejected some light fixtures that were supplied under our contract."

"What's wrong with them?"

"The fluorescent tubes have turned black at the ends."

"Perhaps the *tubes* are defective."

"That's what the fixture manufacturer claims, but the tube manufacturer says the fixture ballasts are defective."

"For heaven's sake, Les, we can't seesaw like this over a few fixtures and tubes. Replace both of them, and let's get on with it. I need this profit for our fiscal year-end!"

"It's not that simple, Phil. There are over a thousand fixtures involved."

"What?"

"Yes, you've heard right."

"Can't we hire some independent testing agency to tell us what's wrong?"

"That has already been done. They think it's the ballast but admit it could be the tubes; however, they won't guarantee it. There are three manufacturers involved for the fixtures, the ballasts, and the tubes, and the testing agency doesn't want a law suit for pointing the finger at the wrong manufacturer."

"Have they tried another manufacturer's tubes?"

"Yes. They turned black, too. Same thing with a different manufacturer's ballasts."

"So, what's your next move?"

"I'm having another meeting tomorrow with everyone involved: the owner's representative, the designers, and each manufacturer's representative. We want to come to the best solution at the least cost to anyone."

"Good luck! Keep me posted."

The next day's meeting was an unhappy event. Everyone pointed a finger at someone else, and everyone produced proof that someone else has had similar problems on other projects. After the manufacturers' representatives were excused from the meeting, the owner's representative turned to me: "It's really your company's problem, Les. Our contract is with your company, not any of the manufacturers."

I didn't comment one way or another.

When I related the meeting to Phil, I could detect in him a rising temper. "Let me think about it for a day, Les."

Sure. But I couldn't think of anything he might come up with to help the situation.

We had lunch together on the next day. "I want to ask you something," he said after we had ordered our coffees. "What do the specifications call for?"

"A one-year guarantee period to replace the defective products," I replied.

"No. I mean regarding the make of the products?"

"The specifications are very explicit. For the fixtures, the ballasts, and the fluorescent tubes they provide the required manufacturer's name and catalogue number."

"And did we ask the engineers to approve alternative products?"

"Yes, we did, but they turned us down."

"I think that's the answer, Les. The engineers wanted certain products. We proposed alternatives, and they turned us down. Now, they want to hold us responsible for their rigidly specified products, which turn out to be defective. We won't stand for that!"

"What're you trying to tell me, Phil?"

"Arrange a meeting with the owner's representative, Les. Make it a lunch meeting at the club, so as to give it a more cordial atmosphere. We'll ask the owner to take us out of the loop – give us a letter of acceptance. I think we can convince the owner to do that, in view of the engineer's rigid specs."

I shook my head in disbelief. How did Phil come up with such ideas? But I arranged the meeting as he had requested. I was lucky to latch onto Jeffrey Goodfellow. Jeff was the owner's senior inspector. He and I had dealings in the past – always on amicable terms, I might add.

"Sure, Les. Just let me grab my calendar. How about Friday?"

"Friday is fine. Can we pick you up?"

"No. I'll meet you at the club. Say twelve?"

"That'll be fine."

Phil and I arrived early at the club. I think Phil needed some fortification. At twelve, I went to the lower lobby to fetch Jeff. Phil and Jeff hit it off extremely well from the outset. For almost two hours, they talked of nothing else than their travels to far-away places – including safaris in Africa and India. I listened raptly, but I was afraid Phil had forgotten why we had arranged this meeting.

Eventually, Jeff looked at his watch and said, "I'm sorry, gentlemen, I have another meeting this afternoon. I gather this was not just a social visit?" He looked at Phil.

Phil sighed. "I sincerely wish it were," he said sadly.

"What's up?"

Phil told him about the light-fixture and fluorescent-tube problem. "The specifications called for these products by catalogue number," he finished, "and our alternative proposals were rejected by the engineers." He gave Jeff a long look.

"I'm surprised at that," said Jeff. "Our engineering manual of requirements explicitly calls for performance specifications for all products."

"Well, in this case, catalogue numbers were specified. We put pressure on the manufacturers to replace these products, but they won't budge. Each is blaming the other for causing the problem. Quite frankly, we don't have enough clout with them. We may never buy their products again."

"What can I do to help?" Jeff wanted to know.

"We would like you to remove the item from our deficiency list and give us a letter of acceptance for the project," Phil said with emphasis.

"Unfortunately, you're the one who has the contract with these manufacturers. We don't have that advantage."

"No, but your engineers have a bigger advantage," said Phil. "They can threaten the manufacturers that their products won't be specified again."

Jeff looked at him for some time. Then he said, "Let me see what I can do, Phil. Give me a few days to look into it, and I'll get back to you."

"Much appreciated, Jeff." We got up to leave and promised each other a repeat luncheon.

On Tuesday the following week, Jeff phoned our office. Phil was out at the time and the call was referred to me.

"How are you, Les?"

"Fine, and you?"

"Fine, too. I called to let you know that your deficiency list is cleared. I'll be issuing a letter of acceptance in a couple of days."

"Great, Jeff. I think Phil will be very happy."

"Give him my best regards, and let him know I'm looking forward to our next get-together."

"I will, Jeff. And thanks!"

"Don't mention it."

16

Cliff Wants an Assessment

Cliff called me at 7:30 one morning. I was just catching up on some work.

"You're in early, Les."

"Yeah. I'm trying to catch up."

"Busy?"

"Moderately. Right now, I'm tying up some loose ends for a project that's finished."

"How long will that take you?"

"Oh, just a few days – a week at the most."

"The reason I'm asking is because I would like you to fly out to the coast. Our Western Division has filed a statement of claim against the owners of a project that was completed three months ago, and I would like you to assess what the value to us might be – for our auditors, you understand?"

"Why did they file a statement of claim? I thought our policy is to negotiate settlements."

"The owners have rejected the claim outright – wouldn't even talk to us – so, we had no choice."

"Can't Walter give you an assessment?" I meant Walter Kemp, the division manager.

"Walter insists that the claim has full value. I don't trust his assessment."

"At what stage are the court proceedings?"

"I believe they are preparing now for depositions in six weeks. Our lawyer has also requested a claims expert's opinion."

"Who is the claims expert?"

"Kasenoff."

"Oh. I had a run-in with one of Kasenoff's engineers once: over a quantification issue."

"All the more reason why I want your assessment of this claim."

"How's Walter going to take this?"

"I'll talk to Walter. He respects your claims experience."

"I think I can make it in about a week, Cliff."

"That'll be fine. Let me have your report as soon as you've reached a conclusion."

Before I left for the coast, I gave Phil a sheet with notes on our various projects, in case something should suddenly come up.

"How long are you going to be away?" he asked me worriedly.

"I hope just a few days, Phil. I'll stay in touch by phone."

Deb, Phil's secretary, made all my arrangements: the flight, a rental car, and my hotel room. Walter met me at the hotel at 3 p.m. and we relaxed in the hotel lounge over drinks.

"Give me some details of the claim, Walter."

He outlined for me a complex pier project: several ships coming in and leaving daily, with all the required facilities for embarking, disembarking, loading, and unloading. Naturally, there were some inevitable construction delays.

"How did you ever get roped into bidding on this project, Walter? This is not your regular line of work, is it?"

No. We had a revenue shortage, and we decided to go for it."

I shook my head. It was a typical dilemma that we had to face occasionally in the construction industry. "Who's the lawyer handling this case for us?" I asked him.

"Jack Frazer."

I knew Jack. He was involved mostly in corporate law. "Jack is not a construction claims lawyer."

"No. He usually handles our general stuff. But he assured me that this is a straightforward claim and he can handle it."

I gave him a doubtful look. I had not yet come across any "straightforward" claims.

"How did you latch onto Kasenoff?"

"It was Jack's idea. He told me his law firm is using them occasionally."

"Have they issued their opinion yet?"

"We should have it by tomorrow – day after, at the latest."

I nodded. "Did you bring me copies of the statements of claim and defense?"

"They're in the envelope, here."

"I also need copies of your estimate for the project and your original claim submission, Walter."

"Okay."

"Who from Kasenoff is rendering the opinion?"

"A chap named Jim Berger."

I didn't know him. "What's his background?"

"He was involved in project management before he came to Kasenoff."

"What kind of project management?"

"I don't know – as an owner's representative, I think."

"Did you run into any shortages during construction?"

"What kind of shortages?"

"Budget shortages, for example."

Walter's face turned red. "Some, but none too serious."

"How low were you below the next bidder?"

"It's hard to say – the owners were considering some alternatives – ten percent, maybe fifteen."

"That's a lot!"

"The other bidders may have allowed too much for contingencies."

"Evidently not, since a claim became necessary." I yawned and excused myself. I didn't feel like beating up on him any longer. "I'll meet you at Jack's office at 10:30 tomorrow morning. Don't forget to bring those copies."

"I'll do that, Les," he said, relieved, and shook my hand.

Before I left for Jack Frazer's office the next morning, I

went over the statements of claim and defense. There was nothing unexpected in either of them: only the usual accusations and denials.

At Jack Frazer's, Walter, Jack and I discussed Jack's plan to proceed and his tentative schedule. "I'm putting a lot of my faith in the claims expert we hired," Jack concluded. "He'll meet us for lunch at the yacht club and bring along his preliminary report."

Jim Berger turned out to be a friendly chap – of medium height, stocky, with a firm handshake. I liked him right away.

"I hear you've been involved in project management, Jim," I said.

"Only as a team member, representing some owners of a power plant in South America," he said modestly.

"That must have been interesting."

"It was, believe *me* – especially having to deal with the available, local labor force!"

"Excuse me, gentlemen," Jack broke in, "I'm rather pressed for time today. Could we have a look at your preliminary report, Jim?"

"Oh, sure." Jim took four copies from his briefcase and handed one to each of us.

I scanned mine quickly. One part caught my eye, and I studied it more carefully. "I see you're establishing production losses by comparing our billings to our labor expenditures, Jim." I looked up at him.

"It's not my preferred method, Les, but I didn't have a choice."

"Why's that?"

"Your supervisors, or rather Walter's supervisors, didn't keep specific performance records with respect to the various tasks completed in the various areas. All we had to go on is the labor expenditures from the cost-accounting system and the billings for the project," he explained. I gave Walter an accusing look, but he pretended to be engrossed in Jim's

99

report.

"Nevertheless, Jim," I said, "this method comes up with some weird production *gains* during the first half of construction."

"I know, but it also, nicely, accounts for the total production loss."

I shook my head in disbelief. Did he really think the owners would be naïve enough to buy an argument based on billings? "I don't think . . ."

"Wait a minute," Jack stopped me, "let me explain something. Jim is going to testify to his opinion. I don't want to influence him in any way. He will be asked specific questions by opposing counsel to determine if there was such influence. Conversely, Jim gave no advice with respect to putting our claim together. His sole purpose is to render an opinion with respect to the causes and the extent of our production losses." He looked at me during this explanation.

"Fine," I said, "I'll talk to you privately after I've had a chance to look at some of the evidence."

Walter and I spent three days going over various documents: jobsite meeting minutes, correspondence with the owners, the estimate, purchase orders, time sheets, and specifications. I wanted Walter with me for two reasons: to speed up getting the information, and to provide him with direct comments on my findings.

I found some evidence of owner-caused production losses, mainly through design changes and delays in providing the required information, but these were minor compared to our shortcomings. From the evidence available to me, our grossly underestimated budget figures, both for materials and for labor, were the cause for most of our production losses.

I phoned Phil that evening to check on things.

"Nothing earth-shaking happened so far," he said. "What did you find?"

"Not much substance to Walter's claim, I'm afraid. I'll

phone Cliff tomorrow, right after I meet with the lawyer. I should be back in two days."

"Okay. See you then."

As I sat across from Jack Frazer the next morning, Jack was visibly nervous. "Why are you involved with this claim?" he wanted to know.

"Cliff Jensen, our president, asked me to give him an independent assessment."

"And did you?"

"I have reached a conclusion, but I have not yet reported it to him."

"May I know what your conclusion is?"

"Sure. I think the owners have caused us some production losses – not enough to take them to court over."

"That's not the opinion of our claims expert, Jim Berger."

"The reason I came to see you is to tell you what I think of his opinion, Jack." He waited. "His method of measuring production," I continued, "may have some validity under different circumstances, which don't apply in our case."

"Tell me more," he prodded.

"Well, if you take the time to examine the expenditures during the first half of the billing period, you'll find two things that go against Jim's argument: first, the billings were substantially inflated and, second, the billings included stockpiled materials that weren't installed until the latter part of construction. Jim is claiming fifty percent completion during this period, based purely on billings, but the actual completion was barely thirty percent. To add insult to injury, Jim is claiming that this fifty percent completion was accomplished at a labor-budget gain and, therefore, the entire project should have experienced a labor-budget gain – all these ridiculous conclusions based on billing percentages!"

"It's pretty hard for the owners to refute his arguments when they are the ones who approved the billings."

"Not at all. Not if they do a proper retro-analysis of the

construction schedule. They'll refute Jim's arguments, Jack, and, when they do, the credibility and justification for our claim will go right out the window!"

"I hope you realize that I need a claims expert's opinion to take this claim to court, Les."

I shrugged. "You could adjust the quantification. That might make the owners more willing to negotiate a settlement."

"But my instructions from Walter are to go after the owners for the full amount of the production loss."

I shrugged again. "Well, I'll give my report to Cliff Jensen and let him take it from there."

I phoned Cliff after lunch and gave him a brief summary of what I had found. "And what's your conclusion?" he wanted to know.

"We don't have a good enough case to proceed to court. The owners will shoot it full of holes, and the judge will dismiss it with costs against us."

"Damn it! I've had a gut feeling that something was wrong!" I didn't respond. "Okay. Send me a brief report of your findings and conclusions, Les. If I need more, I'll get back to you."

Cliff phoned me again a week later. "Jack Frazer still wants to let the case proceed through depositions. He thinks we stand a better chance of settling out of court that way. It's his, Walter's, P & L center, you know. He'll find a way to blame me for losing profit if I interfere too much, Les."

"So, why did you call me?"

"I would like you to sit in on the depositions – try and determine when the owners may be ready to make a deal."

"I don't think I'm allowed to sit in, Cliff."

"Jack Frazer thinks he can convince the owners' counsel to allow it, providing you're strictly an observer."

"When are they starting with depositions?"

"In two weeks."

"Okay, Cliff."

The first two days of Walter's deposition were fairly routine. He testified mainly to the authenticity of a number of documents. On the third day, opposing counsel tore Walter's budget figures to shreds. It didn't take him long to corner Walter into admitting to shortages. "Estimates are never perfect," Walter told him.

We had dinner together at my hotel that evening. Jack said, "Incidentally, Les, you were right about the owners refuting our expert's opinion. They hired another expert, who gave a scathing review of our expert's report. The best we can hope for in that regard is a stalemate."

"You're too optimistic, Jack."

Next morning, opposing counsel attacked our labor units. He said he had it on good authority that some of our labor units were too low. I asked to see Jack for a minute during the next coffee break. "Jack, the last labor unit he attacked is an average labor unit. It's too low for most of the tasks, that's true, but there are some tasks on this project that could be carried out below this average, and I can prove it."

Jack didn't waste any time having a private conference with opposing counsel. When he came back, he said, "We have a settlement offer from the owners."

"How much?"

"About twenty percent." Walter shook his head.

"You'll get less from a judge," I said.

"Cliff will be disappointed," he wailed.

"Let me give him a call," I offered.

When I finally reached Cliff on his cell phone and conveyed the offer to him, he said, "Grab it!"

Walter still looked disappointed, but instructed Jack to draw up the agreement.

17

Phil Studies a Learning Curve

One morning, Phil called me into his office. "Bill is running into a problem on one of his projects," he said.

"What's the problem?" Bill Cawlick was one of our project managers and Phil's protégé.

"The schedule is being delayed by some of the owners' other contractors, and when Bill notified the owners of the low production he's experiencing, they told him this is probably due to the effects of learning curves."

"It probably is, to some extent."

"The problem is, Bill thinks the learning curves have only a minor contribution to the slowdown of production, but the owners disagree. They told him that if production losses are caused by more than the learning curve, Bill should temporarily lay off some workers."

"They are probably correct."

"But if Bill lays off workers, he's going to create other problems for himself."

"So, what do you want me to do?"

"I want you to head out to the site and have a look around – see what the problem really is and what should be done about it." This is normally my job, except that Phil had insisted that he'll look after Bill personally, which would make it his job to investigate these problems on Bill's projects, but he always finds excuses to pawn them off on me. However, I just nodded and assured him that I would have a look at the site tomorrow.

When I arrived at the jobsite, Bill met me at the office trailer and insisted on accompanying me during my walks to various areas. "Sure, Bill. Let's go," I said.

Bill explained to me the various tasks that were being performed in each area. Everybody seemed to be busy, but, as Bill assured me, our performance measurements clearly proved a loss of production.

"Are you comparing these measurements to your budget averages – your labor-unit averages?" I asked him.

He gave me an astonished look that said: What else is there? "Sure," he answered.

These averages incorporated a number of different factors: site conditions, construction conditions and locations, weather conditions, elevations, to name a few, and, of course, the learning curve for each task, which was based on the task's complexity and recurrence. Therefore, comparing production measurements to production averages seldom produced accurate results. Project management usually dissects budget averages and assigns various production quotas to diverse tasks, depending on the conditions under which they are performed, and keeping in mind that these quotas must add up to the averages. However, some project managers, obviously Bill one of them, as a matter of convenience only use the averages in their performance-measurement comparisons, knowing that in the end, after the tasks are completed, the comparison becomes meaningful, and, in the meantime, errors are negligible, since they tend to cancel each other for different tasks – some performed above and some performed below their averages. Nevertheless, this is a guessing game at best, and useless for claim justifications.

"Bill, I think at this stage of construction it is important to get away from your budget averages and assign quotas to diverse tasks, keeping in mind at what stage in the learning curve they are being performed."

"That's a lot of work! It could take several days to accomplish."

"I know that, Bill, but it's the only way if you want to

convince the owners of their responsibility for your losses."

"Well, I don't agree! I'm going to have a talk with Phil."

"You do that," I said and headed over to the owners' office trailer to touch base with George Sulman, the owners' project manager.

George and I had had a few dealings together in the past, and he was glad to see me again. "How're doing, Les? Haven't seen you in ages!"

"Not bad, George. How about you?"

"Still struggling along. What brings you to our site?"

"Phil wants me to have a look around. He's had reports that our production is too low."

"Bill's reports, I bet. I wouldn't pay too much attention to them. We did our own analysis, and we think Bill's out to lunch."

"He says your multi-contractor job conditions are affecting his schedule and production."

"To some extent, yes, I'll agree to that, but his main problem is that he is measuring his productivity inaccurately – he's not making adjustments for construction conditions and for adverse effects of his learning curves."

"I'll recommend to Phil that those adjustments be made, George, but what about Bill's claim that there's interference from other contractors?"

"We're trying to keep that to a minimum, Les, but we're running into the usual coordination problems. Nothing out of the ordinary, though."

"Still, Phil is getting an earful about it from Bill."

"I don't doubt it. I would suggest that you get your measurements straight first. Then report to us any interference out of the ordinary, and we'll see what we can do about it."

"Fair enough, George. I'll probably see you again soon. Take care."

"I'll do that." He got up to shake my hand.

Back at the office, I reported to Phil that Bill was not

measuring his production properly, which prevents him to accurately assess any interference from other contractors. Phil wanted some details.

"Well," I said, "he's comparing everything to our average labor units. If the work is complex, the average labor units are too low, and if the work is simple, they are too high. Also, he's making no adjustments for beginning tasks, when the required labor is much higher than later on, after the wrinkles have been ironed out, as it were."

"You mean this business about the learning curves."

"That's right."

"How easy is it to make these adjustments?"

"It's not hard to do. It just takes a little time to set up at the outset. After that, it's a piece of cake, Phil."

"Then why didn't Bill do this already?"

"Other priorities, I guess."

"I'll talk to him. The adjustments for simple and complex tasks seem straightforward, but how easy is it to make adjustments for learning curves?"

"Harder, because two factors have to be considered: one, simple versus complex tasks, and two, at what stage, time-wise, these tasks are being performed. In the beginning, most tasks take more time to perform; then the time decreases gradually as workers get used to the task and find better ways to perform it. The trick, during measuring performance, is to determine the approximate stage of this learning curve."

"Sounds complicated."

"It's not as bad as it sounds, Phil. All that is usually required is to know when you're at the high end, the low end, or the median – usually the average."

"And what happens if you just go with the average?"

"Not much from our viewpoint – we can live with the inaccuracy – but if you want to make a case for lost production with owners, you'll need the additional accuracy. In Bill's case, I don't think he's got much of a case for a lost-production claim even with more accurate measurements."

"Why's that?"

"Because we knew when we bid on this project that the multi-contractor coordination conditions would produce some hiccups and some lost production. We should've allowed for that factor in our estimate for labor – at least, that's going to be the owners' position."

Phil looked at me for a while, deep in thought. Then he said, "All right. But I still want accurate measurements from Bill. You never know when this comes in handy. All kinds of disruptions and delays could occur on this project."

"I couldn't agree with you more, Phil."

When Bill came in, the three of us had another meeting. Bill voiced his objections to Phil about my suggestion to make proper adjustments to his average labor units. Not only would this take up too much of his valuable time but, also, would it be a total waste of his time.

"I don't agree," Phil told him. "I've made a detailed study of the effects of these adjustments – especially with respect to the learning curves – and I've reached the conclusion that making these adjustments can benefit us in more ways than one."

"But . . ." Bill started to object.

Phil held up his hand. "It's best this way, Bill."

Bill honored me with one of his dirty looks as he walked out of Phil's office. Phil just shrugged as I looked at him.

18

Phil Recommends a Project Agreement

When we landed a mining project that straddled the border of a neighboring state, Phil came to my office with a worried look on his face.

"What's eating *you*?" I asked him.

"Didn't you tell me that the mining project's jurisdiction is with the unions of the neighboring state?"

"Yes."

"Well, I just heard that their contractors are getting ready to settle their terminated agreements with the unions."

"So?"

"I wonder what effect that'll have on us at the mining project."

He was right. We couldn't afford any foul-ups at this stage. "I'll call the secretary of their contractors' association," I said. This, I did promptly. I was told that a special meeting had been called for the following Tuesday at 6 p.m. and, since I had a vested interest, I was welcome to attend. Phil was happy to hear that I intended to do just that.

I flew into the neighboring state's capital next Tuesday morning and checked into one of the better downtown hotels. As I entered the meeting room just before six o'clock, a medium-built, pot-bellied, ruddy-faced man walked up to me with his right hand held out.

"You must be Les Payne," he said. "Welcome to our part of the world. My name is Dale Calderwood. I'm the chairman."

I shook his hand. "Thanks for allowing me to attend your meeting."

"Don't mention it." He stuck his balding pate into the hallway and called out, "Let's get started!"

Two-dozen contractors took their places around a set of tables that were arranged in a square in the middle of the room. Calderwood motioned for me to sit beside him. He introduced me briefly as a visiting contractor who's involved with the new mining project at the border.

Then he cleared his throat and said, "This special meeting is called specifically for the purpose of setting the final guidelines for reaching an agreement with our unions. Because of our dire economic conditions, some of you have suggested to me that we should propose roll-backs to the unions, while others have taken a more realistic stance and suggested roll-overs of the present agreements."

There were calls of "Hear! Hear!" from the crowd.

"I would, therefore, entertain a motion to provide this guidance to our negotiating committee." He looked around the room with his permanently raised eyebrows, which gave him an ever-questioning expression.

Dutifully, one contractor made a motion to roll over the present agreements. Another contractor promptly seconded the motion. Calderwood called for discussion. I held up my right hand. He turned his raised eyebrows toward me in disbelief.

"Mr. Chairman," I said, "my company is looking for concessions from the unions to facilitate our operations at the new mining project."

"Out of the question!" said Calderwood in a domineering tone. "Concessions from the unions would only lead to concessions by us! We can't afford that!" He looked around the room and promptly got more "Hear! Hear!" calls.

I held up my hand again, and he turned his questioning eyebrows on me once more.

"Mr. Chairman, most of you are involved in commercial projects in the cities. The concessions I have in mind involve only out-of-town provisions. These would hardly affect you,

110

and the unions would know that."

"Obviously, Mr. Payne, you have no conception of the tenacity of our unions!" He looked around the room again and got more dutiful "Hear! Hear!" calls. He gave me a sad smile.

I held up my hand again. His smile disappeared. Then he raised his voice and said sternly, "Mr. Payne! You've had your chance twice at discussion! There are members here who deserve a turn!" He looked around the room and got his "Hear! Hear!" responses.

One voice called, "Question!"

Calderwood held up his hand. "The question has been called on the motion before us. All those in favor, say 'aye.'"

"Ayes!" all around the table.

"All those opposed, say 'nay.'"

No nays.

"The ayes have it! The motion is passed unanimously! And that concludes our agenda, gentlemen. The meeting is adjourned."

It was one of the neatest railroading jobs I have ever witnessed.

I went to a pay phone and called Phil. After I related the meeting's outcome to him, he was silent for a few seconds.

"Just let me think for a minute," he said. He actually took a little longer. Then he said, "If I remember correctly, they're past the limit that ties them to collective bargaining. Theoretically, every contractor is one his own and can deal with the unions directly."

"What're you leading up to, Phil?"

"Contact the unions in the morning and set up a meeting with them. Then propose our terms, and ask to give you a project agreement."

"You think they'll go for it?"

"Yes, I do."

I did as he suggested and invited the business managers to join me for dinner at the hotel's private dining room. They all agreed.

111

§

I was stationed at the door as they arrived in groups of two and three. Everybody introduced himself as he walked through the doorway. One chap said, "I'm Jim Culligan. My colleagues have asked me to be their spokesman for this evening." He gave me a handshake and a friendly smile.

"Great!" I said. "Happy to make your acquaintance."

"Likewise, I'm sure."

He sat beside me at the table. The hotel gave us three choices for the main course: chicken, beef, or salmon. Jim advised me on my orders of California red and white wines. The conversation around the table was mainly speculative on the changing economic condition. I was glad of Jim's input. He eased my burden as a host. After the hotel staff served us fruit cocktails and coffees for dessert, I rapped a spoon against my wineglass:

"Gentlemen, may I have your attention, please." The conversation came slowly to a halt. "As you know, my company has been successful in landing the new mining project. However, we don't want to start construction without settled agreements with the unions, and an immediate prospect of that is still a question mark." I paused for effect. I had everyone's attention now. "The project is on a tight schedule, and we can't afford any risks with delays. So, we're proposing to sign a mutually beneficial project agreement with you immediately." I paused again. All eyes were on me. "We're prepared to offer each of you a five percent increase in the wage package for the duration of the project, but we need some concessions to facilitate our operation." I stopped for possible questions.

Jim obliged: "What's the duration of this project?"

"Eighteen months."

"And what are the concessions you're looking for?"

I outlined four issues concerning travel arrangements, camp facilities, and turn-around trips.

"Would you consider paying double time for all overtime?"

Jim wanted to know.

I hadn't expected this question. Overtime was a small factor on this project. Yet, I hesitated. "I think we could agree to that if you gentlemen could agree to a no-strike/no-lockout provision for this project," I said finally.

Jim looked at me for a full thirty seconds and said, "Give us a few minutes will you, Les?"

"Sure thing."

I walked back into the main dining room and ordered another coffee. Jim joined me after about ten minutes. He held out his hand: "You've got yourself a deal, Les." We shook hands on it.

"I'll have the agreement drafted tomorrow morning," he continued. "We'll get together at noon for signatures. How's that?"

"Fine," I said, "much appreciated, Jim."

Next morning, as I finished my coffee after breakfast, Dale Calderwood walked up to my table and sat down, uninvited.

"I hear you've negotiated a project agreement, Les."

"You hear right, Dale."

"We're going to oppose that, you know? With the Department of Labor."

"On what grounds?"

"Unfair labor practice," he said, got up, and walked away.

At noon, I told Jim about Calderwood's threat. He laughed. "Hot air, that's all! The unions won't support that. Your labor practice is about as fair as we've had for a long time. Just forget about it, Les." And with that, he handed me two signed copies of the project agreement.

Back at the office, Phil took ten minutes to scan the project agreement. "You did pretty well getting this agreement, Les – especially the no-strike/no-lockout provision. How'd you manage to get that?"

"I agreed to double time for all overtime."

"But you don't have much overtime on this project."

"Not yet," I admitted.

He looked up and smiled. "I get it," he said. "If the owners want overtime, let *them* pay for it." Phil was quick; make no mistake about it!

"Are you buying lunch?" I wanted to know.

He just smiled and nodded.

19

Phil Suspects a Saudi Deal

Phil and I were relaxing over drinks in our favorite lounge. He had just downed his first double martini, while I was still taking small sips from my glass of a California version of Gewürztraminer. Any subject involving work was the last thing on my mind. We were heading into fall, and my thoughts were wandering to the marshes, where we usually bagged our limit of mallards, and to the wheat fields, where we shot the odd Canada goose. But Phil could seldom get his mind off of work, and this evening was no exception.

He suddenly interrupted my reverie with a comment of which I had missed the last half: "– I want your assessment of this deal, Les."

"Sorry, Phil. What did you say? My mind was elsewhere."

"Hell! How can your mind be elsewhere when you're looking right at me?"

"Sorry, Phil. Truly!"

"Pay attention, will you. I was telling you that I had lunch today with a couple of friends. They were contacted by a sheik from Saudi Arabia. He's proposing a very lucrative partnership to complete some half-finished projects in Saudi Arabia. He has access to these projects through his connection with the king, and he's looking for partners with the expertise to finish them. Apparently, the profit to be made on this deal is measured in the millions. My friends are proposing a joint venture with us, but they suspect that there may be a risk involved that the sheik is withholding. You're good at ferreting out hidden risks, and that's why I want your assessment of this deal." He gave me an expectant look.

I shook my head. "Cliff won't like it, Phil. It's not so long ago since the company lost millions in the Middle East – Iran, I think it was."

"For heaven's sake, Les, we're not proposing to actually undertake any of these projects. I just want you to assess a proposed deal for now. If we don't like the odds, we'll just say 'no' to it."

"So what is it, exactly, you want me to do?"

"My friends are flying to Saudi Arabia to get first-hand information. I would like you to join them."

"When?"

"In about six weeks. It takes that long to get immunizations, passports, visas, et cetera."

"I have a passport."

"It's no good, Les. You were in Israel with it. The Saudis don't like that. You'll have to get a new passport."

"For heaven's sake! What am I getting myself into?"

"Don't get too excited. It's bad for your heart."

"Why don't you go along, Phil?"

"I'm in even worse position than you, Les. The Saudis would probably object to my ancestry."

I gave him an astonished look. "This is getting better and better. Next you'll tell me I'll be meeting up with the Hottentots!"

"It's not quite as bad as that, Les, but I want you to prepare for the worst. I have a friend at Bechtel who can get me a copy of a manual for their employees who are stationed in Saudi Arabia. It's a confidential manual, so treat it with discretion."

I just shook my head and ordered another Gewürztraminer.

When I informed my doctor of my intent to visit Saudi Arabia, he was more than mildly disapproving. He had a list of half a dozen serious diseases for which he prescribed immunizations and warned me that these immunizations might have some bad side effects.

116

"You'll also have to prepare yourself for malaria," he said. "Unfortunately, we have no fool-proof immunization for the disease. I'll prescribe some pills that I want you to start taking immediately and for at least three weeks after you return. They're not a cure, but they'll prevent the worst symptoms from developing."

"Thanks a lot, doc," I said with a rueful smile.

Deb, Phil's secretary, also had her hands full trying to make flight and hotel arrangements. "I'm afraid I can't get you on any direct flights," she informed me.

"Where do I have to stop?"

"London and Paris."

"Why Paris?"

"The London flight to Jeddah takes on more passengers in Paris."

"So I won't even be able to get off long enough to enjoy a girlie show?"

She didn't dignify my comment with a response. "Your companions will arrive in London at different times, but you'll be on the same flight to Jeddah," she added.

I instructed her to get me onto flights that give me an extra day in London and stop in Frankfurt on the way back.

"Why Frankfurt?" she wanted to know.

"I understand that a lot of commerce and transportation for Saudi Arabia is initiated from Frankfurt, and I want to make some contacts in case Phil gets serious about this deal."

She nodded. This made sense to her.

As my departure drew nearer, Phil and I spent more time together. He had done some research of his own, and, judging by his careful coaching, he was plenty worried about my welfare.

"Make no mistake about it, Les, they don't think like we do – the Saudis. I've been doing some reading in Bechtel's manual, and it scares the hell right out of me!" I knew what he meant. I had been reading the same manual.

"Watch yourself, Les," he cautioned me at different times. "When in doubt, do nothing. That's safer than doing the wrong thing." I nodded. I had already reached the same conclusion.

"Did you buy a Koran yet?" he wanted to know. I shook my head. "Do so, but don't take it with you. They don't tolerate translations. God! The more I get into the details, the less I like this deal already."

On the day of my flight to London, Phil did something he'd never done before: He drove me out to the airport. He also gave me some last-minute instructions and a firm handshake. I could be mistaken, but I thought I detected a moist film over his eyes – probably an early sign of a head cold.

I had a whole day to myself in London. The city was as hectic as ever, but I managed to make a few useful contacts. Back at the hotel, my companions Larry Dawson and Al Burton, Phil's friends, had already arrived and had left a message for me to join them in the bar. Larry was a mechanical engineer and Al an air-conditioning engineer, both with extensive project-management experience. They were sitting at a round little table with whiskey-sour drinks in their hands. I sat down and ordered draft ale.

"Going British on us?" said Larry.

"Naw. Just feeling thirsty."

"When did you arrive?"

"Late, last night."

"Been sightseeing a bit?"

"No time. Phil asked me to make some contacts in case the Saudi deal goes ahead."

"Any success?"

"Some. Two people were unavailable."

"Well, I think it's a little premature," Al put in. I didn't disagree.

"When do you want to have breakfast?" I asked them.

118

"Six-thirty," said Larry. "Our flight leaves at nine."

"Any plans for tonight?"

"Al and I have planned to visit a nightclub. You want to join us?"

"I'll pass."

Our flight took off on time, and, after a one-hour stop in Paris, we were on our way to Jeddah. At the Jeddah airport, security personnel with submachine guns greeted us. I was wondering whom they were expecting. The queue at customs moved at a snail's pace, but we finally arrived outside the terminal, where an embassy official met us and drove us to our hotel. He informed us that he had arranged a meeting with the sheik for 10 a.m. the next day. Then he gave us some instructions for proper behavior. His demeanor said: Don't embarrass us. Finally, he asked us if we brought along any medication for diarrhea. None of us did, and he gave us a small vial with twenty or thirty tiny pills in it. "Take these – you might need them," he told us without further explanation.

Next morning at 9:30, the sheik's chauffeur picked us up and drove us to an outlying area of the city. It looked like a slum district to me, and I'm sure it was. As our chauffeur turned into a driveway between two tall hedges, I saw a small, bare-chested, bald-headed, mean-looking Mongol hidden in one of the hedges, no doubt to keep unwanted visitors out.

The two hedges curved along fifty feet of the driveway and then opened to a yard with a one-story compound and an eight-car garage. The buildings looked unappealing as well. A servant led us into the interior of the compound, and what awaited us was pure luxury. We were greeted by the sheik's manager, who took us to a huge room with three sets of soft-leather sofas, each arranged around a low glass table. The sheik, a small, bald-headed fellow, was busy talking into a wireless phone. The manager invited us to sit down at one of the sofa sets, and another servant brought us small cups of green coffee. When the sheik got off the phone, he joined us with a big smile.

"Sorry about that, gentlemen. How was your flight?"

"No complaint."

"And your hotel rooms are comfortable?"

"Yes."

Then he told us that his manager would show us some building sites and inform us of their proposition. "I'll see you in three days," he said smilingly and walked out.

The manager led us back outside, where the car was still running to keep it cool. As we were driving through the city, he pointed out various construction sites and gave us comments as to their location value. I saw no activity at any of the sites and asked him why that was the case. He said that the sites were abandoned by the contractors but didn't offer any details. Late afternoon, as he dropped us off at our hotel, he said that he would pick us up at 6:30 and take us for supper. At supper, when he meticulously explained the various food dishes that covered a long, oval table, I was glad he was there to do it, because I would have thrown caution out the window.

Next morning, the chauffeur picked us up again and drove us to the sheik's offices, where the manager gave us a brief outline of their proposition. He didn't add much to what Phil had already told me, and I asked him to give us some details of the proposed partnership.

"The sheik will be a fifty-percent partner," he said. "The Saudi government requires a minimum Saudi partnership of twenty-five percent, but the sheik decided fifty percent is more equitable because of his valuable contribution."

"What is that contribution?" I wanted to know.

"The king is favoring him with a choice of abandoned construction sites."

"Aren't these sites owned by the Saudi government?"

"I should have said, choice of the ones the government

wants to sell."

"What happens to the ones the government doesn't want to sell?"

"The government will issue contracts for their completion, and our partnership will be invited to bid on them."

"And the properties that the sheik buys?"

"You, gentlemen, will automatically be the ones to finish construction."

"And would the sheik put up fifty percent of the required capital to finish construction?"

"No. The financing for that would be done by you, as your part of the partnership."

"And how would we be paid, eventually?"

"After you complete construction, the sheik will decide whether to sell the property or lease it. If he sells it, his purchase price is deducted first, then all the construction costs that will be paid to you, and the remainder, the profit, will be split fifty-fifty."

"What if there is no remainder?"

"Then nothing would be split, obviously." He gave me a pained look.

I felt sheepish but pressed on. "But supposing there isn't even enough to pay for all of the construction costs?"

"Then there will be a loss, obviously." He smiled the smile of a teacher instructing a schoolboy.

Still, I wasn't satisfied. "And would the sheik split the loss fifty-fifty, as well?"

"No. The loss would be yours, since your construction management may have caused it."

"But that should not be a foregone conclusion. The sales price may also be too low."

He just shrugged. "The sheik is a very good salesman."

"And what about the government contracts – how will they be handled?"

"Just like any contracts: you complete them, the government will pay you for them, and the profit on them is split fifty-fifty."

"And if there is a loss?"

"The loss is yours, obviously. You've prepared the tender, and you have supervised the construction. The sheik had nothing to do with that." He gave me another patient smile.

"And how will the government pay us for the ongoing construction costs?"

"The government makes an upfront deposit in the amount of twenty percent of the contract in trust to an international bank account. Then, twenty percent is deducted from your approved progress billings, and an equivalent amount is released to you from the bank deposit. Should your progress billings include any profit, this is immediately split fifty-fifty with the sheik."

"But supposing that there is a loss in the end, would the sheik pay back his share of the earlier profit taken?"

He shrugged again. "Obviously not. But you don't have to include profit in your progress billings."

I could see now how the Saudis ended up on top and how the sheik had become a billionaire. My companions asked a few more technical questions. Then we thanked the manager, and he had the chauffeur drive us back to our hotel.

After lunch, the chauffeur drove us around the city, following our directions. At one point, we came past a construction site that showed some activity. I asked the chauffeur to stop, and we got out and walked over to the office trailer. A chap by the name of Harry Brown was studying some drawings. He was a civil engineer from Birmingham, England.

"How's your project coming?" I asked him.

"Slowly. We're working with an imported labor force – recruited through a labor broker – mostly unskilled and mostly from Korea."

"How do you get unskilled workers to perform skilled tasks?" I was astonished.

"Patient training," he said. "It's a bugger!"

"I was wondering why so many construction sites are abandoned in Jeddah."

"Two factors: high, double-digit inflation combined with triple the scheduled construction time. It usually breaks contractors halfway through construction."

"But I still see a lot of heavy construction equipment on these sites."

"A Saudi requirement," he said. "You're allowed to import the required construction equipment, but you're not allowed to take it out of the country."

I had heard enough. I looked at my companions, and both shrugged. I think they had heard enough as well.

Next day, we kept our appointment with the sheik. He pointed to a corner of the huge room as we walked in. A portable bar was located there. I'm sure it hadn't been there three days previously. My companions helped themselves to a drink. I sat down at one of the sofa squares, and a servant put a glass of tea in front of me – probably because I didn't finish the green coffee last time I was here.

The sheik looked at me. "Have you reached any conclusions?" he wanted to know.

"It's not our place to reach conclusions," I replied. "We're here on a fact-finding mission. Our principals will reach the conclusions.

He looked disappointed. "But, surely, you must have some thoughts yourself!"

I did. But not to be expressed at this time, I determined. "No, only some scrambled facts, which I have to sort out and formulate into a readable report for my principals."

My companions had the good sense to hover by the portable bar rather than to join us with their drinks. The sheik ignored them, perhaps to show his contempt for their foul addiction. "When will I hear from you?" he said.

"Within a week of our return."

He nodded and walked out of the room.

§

My companions flew back to London the next day, and I decided to go through with my planned stop in Frankfurt, just to complete my investigation, although I doubted that Phil would make use of the information. Deb had booked me into a hotel near the main railway terminal, for convenience, but the place was third-rate: a common bathroom, my window facing an airshaft, starched towels, and a lumpy, down bedcover. Everything I hated with a passion. To top it, their offer of continental breakfast consisted of burnt toast and bitter coffee. This put me in the frame of mind to waste no time making my contacts and heading back to the airport.

On the flight back home, I sat beside a fellow who had spent a couple of years in Saudi Arabia. The Saudis had asked him to leave for some misbehavior, on which he didn't elaborate, and he told me a few stories that made up my mind to stay home, where I belong.

Phil had a big smile on his face. "Man, with all the bad news from the Middle East, I'm happy you're back in one piece," he said. He kept shaking his head while I gave him a complete report, especially as I came to the part of splitting profits but not losses with the sheik. "No way, José!" he said. "Can you imagine what head office would say to your risk analysis for a prospective project with that profit-and-loss-split provision?"

"I can imagine what head office would say to my risk analysis even without that profit-and-loss-split provision!"

"I suspected something fishy, but this profit-and-loss split is worse."

"Yeah. I christened it the Saudi partnership factor: Heads, *we* win, tails, *you* lose."

Phil laughed. "Well put!"

20

Phil Likes a Bahamian Project

"Got time for a drink, tonight?"

I looked up from my spreadsheet at Phil standing in the doorway to my office with a cup of coffee in his hand.

"What's up?" I wanted to know.

"Why should anything be *up*, Les? I asked you a simple question."

"Yeah. I'm free."

"Good," he said, and walked away.

"I want to run an idea past you," said Phil as we relaxed over our drinks.

"Shoot."

"This architect friend of mine told me about a project he's designing for the Bahamas."

"What kind of project?"

"A casino hotel."

"So, what's your idea?"

"Do you think head office would let us construct it?"

"I doubt it."

"Why not?"

"It's not our line of work."

"We could claim we are responding to a special invitation from the architect."

"Do you have an ulterior motive, Phil?"

"Well, it would provide us with a few badly needed holidays – supervising this project, I mean."

"Head office will probably suspect that's what it's all about."

"We could suggest that Cliff should visit the project during construction. He'll actually be closer to it than we."

I shook my head. "I'll prepare a risk analysis when this project comes out for tender, if that's what you want, but I doubt if the board committee will approve it, Phil."

"It would depend on how it's presented to the board members, wouldn't it?"

"I suppose so."

Two months later, the project came out for tender, and we were invited to submit a bid. Phil encouraged me to prepare a risk analysis for head office immediately. I knew head office would be particularly critical of this project, so I took extra care to address the areas in the risk analysis that I suspected would get the board committee's attention. My enquiries about the labor force uncovered the slow pace of construction in the Bahamas, with a resulting loss of production, and I made sure this issue was properly addressed. Also, I went into some detail about the shipping problems that we may encounter with the required construction materials and equipment.

When Phil scanned my draft before I submitted it to head office, he wanted to know if I had intended to scare the board committee members.

"I just want to make sure they don't accuse us of overlooking some of the obvious risks, Phil."

He nodded. "Okay. Send it off. Let's see where it leads us."

A week later, we received an invitation from head office to attend a board committee meeting. Phil and I were discussing our strategy over lunch.

"What do you think will be their main objection to this project, Les?"

"Our inexperience with this type of construction."

"How did you address that in your risk analysis?"

"I have a friend, a project manager, who has experience

with this type of construction and is willing to manage the project for us."

"That's great! You haven't mentioned that before."

I shrugged. "I put the possibility in my risk analysis, but he actually confirmed his availability only yesterday."

"That's great, Les. That should clinch it for us with head office."

"I sure hope so, Phil."

We arrived at head office just before 10 a.m. on the day of the appointed meeting with the board committee. The receptionist took us into the big boardroom, where a coffee urn had already been prepared. Phil and I helped ourselves to a cupful of the hot brew and sat down at the end of the long table.

Cliff arrived with two committee members ten minutes later. "I believe you know Jack Osborn and Harry Linquist."

Mr. Osborn nodded to us and sat down. Mr. Linquist came over to shake hands with us: "Good to see you again."

Cliff sat down and looked at my risk analysis. Each of his board members did likewise, as if they had never seen it. Phil and I just studied their expressions for any revealing signs. No such luck.

After five minutes, Cliff looked at Phil. "What's so special about this off-line, off-shore project, Phil?"

"We're just responding to an architect's invitation, Cliff."

Cliff nodded. This happened all the time. He looked at me. "You've done a pretty thorough job evaluating the risks, Les." I had the feeling that this was just an introduction to something I had probably missed, but I nodded. "Except for one thing," he continued. Here it comes. "You've played down the currency issue."

"I didn't think there was much of an issue, Cliff. The Bahamians have tied their currency to the US currency; it hasn't fluctuated for some time."

"I'm surprised to hear you say that, Les. Are you trying to tell us that tying a currency to the US currency eliminates all risks?"

Frankly, I hadn't given it much thought, but before I could answer him, Mr. Linquist said, "Let me get this straight, Cliff. Do I understand correctly that we will be paid in Bahamian dollars?" Cliff acknowledged this. "I thought a Miami consortium is building this complex," Mr. Linquist continued.

Cliff said, "You're correct, in part, but there are also partners from Nassau – even the Bahamian government has an interest in it, I believe." He looked at me and I nodded.

"That throws a whole new light on this project!" Mr. Osborn gave me a mean look.

"Hardly, sir," I said. "My risk analysis contains a detailed description of the ownership makeup."

"Yes, we have that," said Cliff, "but you have neglected to give us a proper risk analysis of the Bahamian currency, Les."

"Quite frankly, Cliff, I hadn't put a high risk factor on their currency because it has been tied to the US currency for some time."

"That's rather presumptuous of you, isn't it?" said Mr. Linquist. "Do you remember what happened to the Canadians a while back?" He continued to answer his own question. "They had their currency tied to the US currency, but it put an unnatural strain on their economy, and when they finally cut their currency loose, it dropped quite considerably."

I nodded. He was right, of course. "Do you think the Bahamian economy is as weak as that, sir?" I responded lamely.

"That's hardly the point," said Cliff. "It's your job to provide *us* with that answer in your risk analysis, not to ask *us* questions that *you* should have researched."

I could have crawled into a hole. Not only did I feel inadequate, but I also felt ashamed of Cliff's rebuke.

Mr. Osborn again: "The fact of the matter is, we don't speculate on foreign currencies – we deal in the US currency."

"We could hedge the Bahamian currency," I suggested.

"Hedging is costly and brings along a multitude of problems," said Cliff. "For one thing, you always have problems fitting it into the time frame you want. We've had bad experience with that in the Middle East."

"What about the labor force?" Mr. Osborn asked.

I was on surer footing here. "We're obliged to hire local labor first, sir; when local labor becomes unavailable, we can import our labor. However, there is no restriction on supervisory staff." Apparently satisfied, he nodded.

"I see you've done a fair job evaluating the potential production loss on that account," put Mr. Linquist in.

"Yes. We've had some statistics to go on." This seemed to satisfy him.

"When is this tender closing?" asked Cliff.

"Three weeks from now."

"Yes, I see it. Well, I think we have enough information for now. If we need more, you'll hear from us. We'll give you our decision in a week to ten days."

Neither of them asked Phil another question, and Phil didn't volunteer to come to my help either.

When we were settled down in a taxi on the way to the airport, Phil said sadly, "I think we can forget about that project."

"I suppose. I had no idea they would focus their concerns on the Bahamian currency, Phil."

"It would have made no difference, even if you had, Les."

"You've been to the Bahamas, Phil; did you have any concerns about their currency?"

"No, not with the few dollars I spent there. But I can understand Cliff's concern with millions of dollars at stake."

"I suppose you're right. So, what do we do next?"

"Let's just wait until we hear from them."

A week later, Cliff sent us a memo: "You may proceed with the Bahamian project providing you qualify your tender to state that it is based on US currency and providing that you demand to be paid in US currency."

"There you have your instructions, Les," said Phil as he handed me the memo. "I'm surprised they let us submit a tender at all!"

And submit a tender we did – with Cliff's qualifications. And the owners promptly rejected it. Phil's architect friend refused to comment until contracts were signed. Then, he told Phil "confidentially" that the tenders were very close – ours was actually low – but that the owners had decided to accept an unqualified tender from a Nassau contractor.

Phil said to me, "I wonder who'll be the winner in that deal?"

"I don't know, but I do know who's the loser."

21

Phil Offers Sound Advice

I was sitting behind my desk with my eyes closed; when I opened them, I looked straight at Phil, sitting in a chair at the opposite wall, a cup of coffee in his hand, and a smile on his face: "Having a little snooze?"

"No," I said, "I'm thinking about a reconciliation method with respect to our production loss in the last claim against PetroHi-G."

"How do you propose to reconcile that?"

"As you know, we've been successful in identifying individual production-loss causes, which we quantified as they occurred." He nodded. "Well," I continued, "I don't want the owners to accuse us of padding these quantifications, since we've included impacts on our original work. Furthermore, we've also had a few shortcomings that are known to the owners." He nodded again. "So, I took the total labor-cost overrun and adjusted it by estimated labor amounts for our shortcomings, and I was able to reconcile that with the individual loss quantifications."

"In other words, you're comparing the individual loss quantifications with a modified total cost."

"Exactly."

"But how can you separate the impact on the extra work from the impact on the original work?"

"Unfortunately, I'm unable to pinpoint these impacts with either method – they remain an estimate."

"In that case, I think the owners will be suspicious regardless which method you employ in your quantification."

"Yes, but since both methods yield the same results, which,

do you think, is the better method to base the claim on? The other method I can always use later, during settlement negotiations."

"Well, if you use the individual quantifications, you're going to be accused of covering up your shortcomings. With the modified-total-cost method, at least you're identifying your shortcomings and making adjustments for them."

"Although the quantification of the shortcomings can also be challenged, and the amount of impact on the original work remains an issue."

"Well, let's get out of here. We can discuss it some more over lunch."

After we ordered our drinks, Phil said, "Claim negotiations are the toughest negotiations – even tougher than labor negotiations."

I didn't respond.

"The reason is," he continued, "that we ask the owners to pay for an intangible benefit – you can even call it a penalty, if you like. It would help if you could show the owners that they actually received a tangible benefit."

He looked at me for a minute to make sure I was following him. He got himself into one of his pedantic moods.

"That's one of the keys to negotiations, in any case," he continued. "After you determine what it is you want, you'll have to find a way for the other party to help you get there – always see things from the other party's viewpoint, if you get my meaning."

"Do you have much experience with claim negotiations, Phil?"

"Actually, no. I'm not good at negotiations. I know what has to be done, mind you, but when I'm called upon to do it, it's as if I'm dumbstruck. But I've been in negotiation sessions, as part of a team, and I've observed some of the principles first-hand."

I nodded. This made sense to me. I've seen Phil strike out

132

with Cliff; yet, he had described to me beforehand the winning tactics that he was later unable to carry out.

"I find it hard to imagine how, from another's viewpoint, I can reach my goal, Phil."

"It's never easy, especially in claim negotiations. That's why many contractors use the hat-in-hand approach: We've done a fine job for you; won't you help us cover our losses? It works surprisingly often."

"Do you have any examples of reaching your goal from the other's viewpoint?'

"I should have. Let me think." He was silent for a while. "Yes. A project comes to mind that was delayed fifteen days by the owners at the start of construction. We managed to accelerate the work and finish the project on time. Then, we submitted a claim for lost production, additional supervision, and so on, due to the acceleration. The owners disputed the claim. During settlement negotiations, we demonstrated to the owners that, had we not accelerated the work, and had the project been completed fifteen days later, the owners would have lost an operational profit of ten times the amount of our claim. That did the trick. The owners settled without further objections." He smiled at me, as if to say, see what I mean?

"Interesting. But really not applicable in our case."

"No. You wanted an example of seeing things from the owners' viewpoint. The main thing to remember is that someone's loss is usually someone else's gain, and if you can demonstrate this gain you're seeing things from the other's viewpoint, as it were."

"But often negotiations deteriorate on moralistic issues, as each side points out the other's wrongdoing."

"Sometimes, you can overcome that by agreement." He finished the last of his double martini. "I'll give you an example. During one settlement negotiation session that I recall, the owners accused our supervisors of failing to measure up to the task. 'We don't disagree,' I told them, 'but our supervisors were planning for different conditions; you have loaded them up with extra work that more than doubled our original contract; this extra work was added sporadically, which created the problem with appropriate adjustments: for the workforce, additional construction equipment, additional materials, and so on. Towards the latter part of construction, our workforce was nearly triple of the one we had originally anticipated and planned for. Even if our supervisors didn't measure up to the task, as you claim, it is surprising how well they coped with it to complete your project without a major delay.' After that, the owners pretty well refrained from further accusations." He took a sip from a new martini. "Right and wrong are strange concepts," he continued. "If I dropped you in some part of London without telling you which city you're in, you would assume that the drivers are on the wrong side of the street. Again, it depends on the viewpoint." He smiled at me. "So, before you put up, or buy into, an argument, make sure you've got the viewpoint straight."

As we were heading back to the office, Phil said, "There's another important negotiating tactic I should mention." He looked at me to make sure I was paying attention, and I raised my eyebrows to accommodate him. "Whether or not you're successful," he continued, "depends a lot on how you present your proposition." He stopped for effect and looked at me. I kept my eyebrows raised. "Let me give you another example," he continued. "I once heard a story that is worth repeating: A chain-smoking young priest went to the father, confessed to his addiction, and asked the father if he could smoke while he was praying. The father looked disgusted and said, 'Certainly not!' Two years later, another chain-smoking young priest came to the father and said, 'Father, I have a confession to make: I'm a chain-smoker; sometimes the spirit grabs me and I must pray immediately. Do you think it's okay if I pray while I'm smoking?' The father gives this some thought. 'Yes, I think that'll be okay.' Do you see what I mean?" He looked at me as I laughed.

22

Cliff's Involvement in a Claim

We had already submitted and settled several claims against PetroHi-G for various phases of their upgrader, but on the last claim, the largest one, PetroHi-G's engineers put up some unusual opposition. Although they had offered us a settlement amount of just over a million dollars, it was barely twenty-five percent of our claim request; in meeting after meeting with them, we were unable to convince them to improve their offer. At the same time, we had pressure from head office to settle this claim. Phil told me that head office had a temporary cash-flow problem.

Cliff phoned me one morning to inquire about the status of our negotiations.

"It hasn't improved any in the past month, Cliff."

"I think I'll give PetroHi-G's senior vice president a call and see if I can speed things up."

"I wonder if he's going to see this as a sign of weakness."

"How do you mean?"

"Well, in these type of negotiations, it's best not to appear too anxious."

"I'll try not to give that appearance, Les."

"Okay, Cliff."

Cliff phoned me again, two days later. "I talked to Oliver Bradley; he said the blame for our losses lies mostly with us, and that's why they're unwilling to up their settlement offer. Also, if we want to accept their offer, we can have payment within two weeks. I like the latter."

"Well, accusations are cheap, Cliff. I can assure you, they

wouldn't stand up in court."

"I don't have the luxury of putting this to the test, Les. Can you suggest something else?"

"I'm not suggesting that we should take them to court, Cliff."

"I know that. So, how do we handle the situation to get payment as fast as possible?"

"Do you mind if I have a talk with Oliver Bradley?" Oliver Bradley was, after all, on Cliff's level, and good protocol demanded that I should deal only with Mr. Bradley's staff.

"Be my guest," said Cliff. He must be desperate.

"Would you mind calling him and suggesting it, Cliff?"

"No. I'll call him."

"I'll let you know how I've made out."

"Do it as soon as possible, Les."

"Sure."

Deb set up a meeting for the following Tuesday. I arrived at Oliver Bradley's office ten minutes early, and he let me wait until the appointed time. His greeting was almost hostile, which made me careful not to start on the topic of our meeting. Fortunately, he led our conversation into a different channel: We talked for almost half an hour about our travel experiences.

Finally, he asked me, "What did you want to see me about, Les?" His manner was friendly enough, but I detected an apprehension.

"I want to gain a better understanding of how you've arrived at the amount of your settlement offer."

"That's simple, Les. We disagree with your quantification. However, we know we've caused you some problems, and we decided to offer you twenty-five percent of your claim."

"Do you mind telling me *why* you disagree with our quantification?"

"I don't want to get into an argument with you, Les."

"I'm not here to give you any arguments, Oliver. I'm here

136

to get information."

"Well, your quantification method uses the modified-total-cost approach. We think that's too subjective. Aside from a few admissions of shortcomings, you've spread your impact not only over the extra work but also over the total original work. We think that's not justified because some of the original work was not impacted."

"Would you be willing to negotiate the amount of original work that was impacted, in your opinion?"

"We would certainly be more receptive to that approach. Your present method is not acceptable to us, Les."

I nodded. "Can we meet again in a week or two? I want to think this over and come up with a new approach."

"Certainly. Give me a call when you're ready."

"Cliff may want to come as well."

"You're both welcome."

We talked for a few more minutes about our travels and parted as friends.

"I enjoyed our meeting, Les. I had expected a more antagonistic attitude from you. Look forward to seeing you again," he said as I walked out.

Before I boarded my flight back, I phoned Cliff and gave him a brief report on the meeting.

"I don't see how you've made any progress," he said.

"Oh, but I have, Cliff. I've established which method of production-loss quantification is acceptable to Oliver Bradley, and that's a big step forward."

"You're the claims expert, Les, but I fail to see how Bradley's method differs all that much from yours."

"It doesn't, in the final analysis, but it gives us a better tool to convince him to up his offer."

"Would you mind explaining to me how you reach that conclusion?"

"Not at all. Oliver Bradley thinks that our modified-total-cost method allows too much impact on our original contract work and that this method hides the impact. With his method, we would assign full impact on all the extra work and a lesser, negotiated amount of impact on the original contract work."

"How would the result differ?"

"That depends on the negotiated percentage of impact on the original contract work."

"How much would that lose us?"

"Hopefully, only twenty-five percent."

"So, what's your next move?"

"It'll take me about a week to design a computer model that incorporates all the claim factors and assigns given percentages of impact to the extra work and the original work. Then I'll print out spreadsheets for the different percentage scenarios. At the meeting with Oliver Bradley, after he agrees on a percentage for the impact on the original work, I'll pull out of my briefcase the appropriate spreadsheet and demonstrate to him what settlement amount he should be offering us based on this percentage."

"Sounds simple."

"Nothing is simple when it comes to claims, Cliff, but I think my plan will convince him to increase his present offer quite substantially."

"When are you planning to meet with Bradley again? I'd like to join you if it fits into my schedule."

"I'll be ready in a week. So, any time after that."

"How about the following Thursday, ten days from now?"

"Suits me, but I'll have to confirm it with Oliver Bradley. I'll let you know as soon as I have it confirmed."

"Fine. And please call me when your computer model is finished. I like to know the results of the different scenarios."

"Sure thing, Cliff."

For the next few days, I closed my office door to minimize interruptions. However, Phil paid me regular visits. On the third day, he said, "How's it coming, Les?"

"I'm just about there, Phil. I'm just in the process of

reconciling all the figures and testing for potential bugs."

"The biggest bug is that we'll have to drop our original claim amount, no matter what!"

"True. But it's the only solution to a fast settlement."

"We wouldn't need a fast settlement if it weren't for Cliff's cash-flow problem."

"Why don't you take that up with him? Perhaps he'll agree on some concessions for the coming year."

"I will! You can place a bet on it!" he said and walked out.

I took another day playing with the computer model. I've learned long ago that it pays to try out all possible scenarios until I'm sure there are no more bugs. Then I phoned Cliff and gave him the results.

"What's the best settlement you're hoping for, Les?"

"Well, as I told you last week, I'll try to commit him to a percentage – that'll automatically produce the amount he should be offering us. If I'm successful, it should be in the range of three times his present offer. Still, it'll only be seventy-five percent of our claim amount."

"I'm desperate enough to settle for less than that."

"I hope you don't show your desperation at the meeting next Thursday, Cliff."

"Have no fear."

Our meeting with Oliver Bradley started again with an exchange of travel experiences – this time, Cliff's, since he did most of the traveling.

At an appropriate pause, I said, "I've been thinking about your method of approaching the impact quantification, Oliver."

"And what conclusion did you reach?"

"Would you allow us one-hundred percent of the experienced impact on extra work and seventy-five percent on our original work?"

He gave a quick response, "No. Seventy-five percent is too

high. A fair value is less than that."

"Sixty-five percent?"

"Less."

"What, then?"

"Fifty percent. No more!"

I looked at Cliff, he shrugged, and I opened my briefcase and took out a spreadsheet. I looked at it for a minute and shook my head. "According to my calculations, Oliver, that would cut about twenty-five percent off of our claim."

"May I see that?"

I handed him the spreadsheet. Now *he* looked at it for a minute and shook his head. "My board won't buy this," he said to me.

"Why? Is there something wrong with my figures?"

"No, no. It's just that it exceeds my limit." When I didn't respond, he turned to Cliff. "Can I have a word with you, Cliff?"

Cliff nodded, and both got up and left the room. I sat alone for nearly half an hour, reading the latest *Time* magazine. Then, Cliff came back and said, "Let's go." I got up and followed him to the elevator lobby. As we walked away from the PetroHi-G Building, he said, "The claim's settled."

"You mean he went for the figure in my spreadsheet?"

"No. He offered me two-thirds of that. That's what took so long. I had one hell of a time convincing him to go higher."

"So, where did you end up?"

"He finally agreed to a figure which is about sixty-eight percent of our original claim amount."

"I think I could've convinced him to give us the seventy-five percent in my spreadsheet."

"I don't think so, Les. He's got his own political problems. If you force him into a corner, he's going to come out fighting. Besides, we need him to support us on future projects. In any case, he's solved my problem."

I nodded. Obviously, the upper echelon is looking out for its members.

23

Phil Wants More Unearned Revenue

Phil had a regular habit of interrupting my work. One day, he walked into my office, sat down, and slurped from his cup of coffee. "Are you wondering, sometimes, why our other divisions consistently win awards for outstanding return on net assets?" he said in a complaining voice.

"I haven't given it much thought. I suppose their asset requirement is lower than ours; or, their profits may be higher than ours."

"You're only partially correct, but the RONA [return on net assets] can also be manipulated, even if the profit is low."

"How's that?"

"One way, probably the easiest way, is to overbill your projects." What he meant was that, in our monthly progress billings, we should increase the cost of materials delivered and the labor to install them – thus, creating unearned revenue.

"But we're doing that, too, Phil."

"Only to offset holdbacks. No, I mean *really* overbilling them! In some cases, this not only cuts down on the asset requirement, but it may even result in negative assets. In other words, the division becomes an asset supplier." Holdbacks are the amounts withheld from monthly progress payments, usually ten percent, to satisfy local lien legislation.

"It would take quite some convincing to get the owners to approve such huge overbillings."

"Yes, but I think you could do it, Les. Why don't you give it a try?"

§

There are only a few projects that lend themselves to extensive overbillings – usually projects with a high material and a low labor content – and we had one of these coming up. However, if the owners' project manager is sharp and suspects the contractor's intent, he will be very critical of all billings.

I had earmarked a project for my overbillings that was managed for the owners by Craig Horton. Craig was sharp but rather lax when it came to approvals of progress billings. He was more interested in completing his project on time than in creating conflicts over trivial matters, such as billing amounts. Nevertheless, he did question the amounts, and he required signed statements guaranteeing that the billing amounts accurately reflect the materials delivered to the jobsite and the labor expended to install them. I was uneasy about this guarantee, simply because I'm always claim conscious.

One evening when Phil and I were relaxing over drinks, I mentioned this to him. He said, "You worry too much, Les. Do you have any reason to believe that there might be a claim?"

"Now that you mention it, yes, I have. The project is starting to slow down because of missing information coming from the owners, and it looks like we may get an abnormal amount of extra work."

"Why don't you cover any production-loss impacts in your quotes for the extra work?"

"Craig Horton will only buy that if I can demonstrate that we're losing production, and I can't demonstrate that while I'm trying to prove to him that we're more complete than we actually are – for my overbillings. You see what I mean?"

"I do, but that's not yet the case, is it?"

"Not yet, but I'm afraid it might develop soon. Why couldn't we manipulate the RONA in other ways?"

"Such as what?"

"Well, we could withhold payments to our suppliers for another month."

"That might slow down their deliveries."

"How about reducing fixed assets and inventories?"

"Same answer, Les. Most of our fixed assets consist of tools and construction equipment that you need to get the job done on time. And our inventories help speed up the deliveries of certain materials that are slow in coming from the suppliers."

I nodded. He was right, of course. "You're right, Phil. Tell me, how much of a benefit, other than an award, are we really getting from our overbillings?"

"Head office is charging us ten percent per annum on the average assets employed by us. The more successful we are in lowering this average, the more we save, and the savings go right to the bottom line – the profit."

"Does head office pay us the same percentage if we come up with negative assets through our overbillings?"

"Yes. The formula takes care of that automatically."

I was impressed. No wonder that our other divisions were striving for that.

"Satisfied?" he wanted to know.

"Not quite. What if we lose a claim that outweighs these ten-percent savings on the average assets?"

"We'll cross that bridge when we come to it, Les."

"Okay. I just hope there'll be a bridge to cross."

"Don't worry so much."

And Craig Horton allowed me to be very successful in my overbillings. But one day, when the project was about fifty percent complete and I had already billed seventy percent, he called me into his office.

"I'm concerned, Les," he said. "According to your billing percentage, you're ahead of the schedule, but my schedulers tell me that you may not be as far advanced as you claim. I know their schedule updates are a little behind, but I reckon I should get it straight from the horse's mouth. What do you have to say?"

"I think you've answered your own question, Craig: Your schedulers are behind."

He nodded. "And you're sure you're seventy percent complete, Les?"

"Close to it, Craig."

He nodded again. "Okay, but don't come complaining to me if you have to accelerate the work to complete the project on time."

I just looked at him. Gosh, he had an excellent intuition. My thoughts were already proceeding along the same lines.

I wasted no time bringing Phil into the picture. "I think I have to accelerate the work to complete the project on time, Phil."

"Can you charge for that?"

"No."

"How much will it cost?"

"A bundle."

He knew what I meant. We had a number of acceleration claims in the past. "Can we reverse our overbilling trend?" he wanted to know.

"Too late for that. We are only fifty percent complete, and we've overbilled forty percent."

"Wow!"

"Yeah."

"I think you'll have to revert to actual-cost billings from now on."

"Won't do. I'll have to revert to sixty percent of actual-cost billings from now on."

He looked astonished.

"Look at the arithmetic, Phil. I have to squeeze fifty percent of the cost into thirty percent of the billings."

He nodded. "Of course! I just hope that that won't nullify your earlier overbillings."

"It will, to some extent. I just hope it won't nullify a possible claim for slowdowns." But even as I said it, I knew it would.

§

I decided to put this to the test. When I had lunch with Craig, two days later, I asked him, casually, if the project's budget could stand some reimbursement for the time lost by the tardy information flow.

He gave me a surprised look. "I don't think you're suffering, are you, Les?"

"I could be doing better with prompt information."

He shook his head. "You're way ahead of schedule, Les. I don't see how our information flow has slowed you down. Besides, we're very generous with your quotes on extra work."

I let it go. Sometimes, one has to know when to leave well enough alone. I was just hoping that the slowdown impacts on our work would be covered by the extras. Craig was right, he didn't give us much of an argument on the pricing for the extra work.

But it didn't take long to become apparent that our budget for labor was going to overrun, especially since I had to start accelerating the work to complete the project on time.

I decided to have another discussion with Phil. "Our labor budget is definitely going to overrun, Phil, and I can't make a case with Craig Horton to pay me for slowdowns."

"Can you make a case for acceleration?"

"No. My overbillings took care of *that*!"

"How much of a loss are you expecting?"

"Seven or eight percent of the labor and the labor-related overhead."

He whistled. "Did you pick up any savings in your material purchases?"

"Some. Not enough to cover more than half of the labor overrun."

He looked glum. "The reduced charges from head office on our average assets will barely cover the other half, Les."

I nodded. I had already come to the same conclusion. "So,

what do we do, Phil?"

"I guess we'll have to bite the bullet, Les."

I nodded again. "There is a saving grace, though."

"What's that?"

"We'll be honored by head office with an award for outstanding performance in the return on net assets."

His faint smile disappeared, and he grimaced in disgust.

24

Phil Supports a Bonus Scheme

One day, over lunch, I was telling Phil that I had an idea that might increase our production quite substantially. Such ideas always caught his undivided attention.

"Tell me about it, Les."

"Well, it's a bonus scheme."

"There are lots of those around, Les."

"Yes, but this one is different. This one is not paid from production savings. It is paid to workers regardless of production."

Now I really had his attention. "Tell me more."

"There's not much more to tell, Phil. The worker gets his wages, as per union agreement. So the union can't complain. Then, for every unit of work he installs, he gets a bonus. The only time he gets no bonus is when he installs nothing."

"How much of a bonus do you have in mind?"

"I have not yet completed my calculations in that regard, but I'm thinking in terms of ten percent of the labor budget."

"Can your estimates stand an increase of ten percent in the labor budget?"

"That's just it, Phil, I wouldn't allow any increases in the labor budget."

He gave me a look of total disbelief. "Surely you're joking, Les?"

"No. I'm dead serious. The bonus would be completely outside of the budget."

"Then where's the money for it coming from?"

"From anticipated savings in the labor budget."

"But I thought you said the worker gets a bonus whether or

not he installs the number of units estimated for a day's work."

"He will."

"So?"

"So, I'm anticipating that the bonus will give him an incentive to install more units than estimated."

"But if you're paying out bonuses amounting to ten percent of your labor budget, what makes you think that production will increase by ten percent or more?"

"I don't know that for sure, Phil. It's a speculation on my part. Human nature, you know. The natural greed of people will make them produce more to get a higher bonus."

"And what happens if your ten-percent figure is wrong?"

"It's a calculated guess on my part. If it's wrong, we adjust it on the next project."

"So, we could experience a loss on the first project?"

"We could, but I believe it's unlikely, Phil."

He thought about this while he finished his New York steak. "It's absolutely ingenious, Les. Of course, we'll have to get permission from head office to implement the scheme, but I'll support you one-hundred percent."

"Thanks, Phil. I'll ask Cliff if he can spare us some time next week, when we're at head office for the discussions on the northern mining project."

"Do that. Did you send in your risk analysis yet?"

"I have."

"Do you expect any opposition from the board committee?"

"Not much. The only risk is a shortage of manpower up there."

"That'll be enough to make them nervous."

"But every contractor will have the same problem."

"Yeah. You're right."

Cliff had readily agreed to extend our meeting by half an hour. He, too, was always interested in new ideas to improve production.

Phil and I had arrived early at head office. The receptionist took us into the big boardroom, where an urn with hot coffee was already waiting. Promptly at 10 a.m., Cliff walked in with two board members. "You know Harry Linquist," he said, "and Frank Gladstone is taking Jack Osborn's place today."

"How are you, Mr. Linquist?" I said, shaking hands.

"Good. I thought I told you to call me Harry?"

"Harry."

"Call me Frank," said Mr. Gladstone, as I shook hands with him. He was a youthful, sixty-year old gentleman, with a happy expression.

The three board members took five minutes to look through my risk analysis for the northern mining project. Cliff was the first to comment.

"You've identified a local manpower shortage as the main risk, Les."

"That's right. We can expect to get only about twenty-five percent of the required labor locally, the rest will have to be imported."

"At what additional cost?" Harry wanted to know.

"I expect only additional cost for initial, rotational, and return travel expenses."

"Excuse my ignorance, but what are rotational travel expenses?"

"Every month, we'll have to fly the workers out to spend a few days with their families and then fly them back again."

"I see. Won't that add a substantial amount to the overall cost?"

"It will. However, all our competitors will have to allow the same."

"What about accommodations up there?" Frank asked.

"The owners are providing a camp free of charge, except for days over the estimate."

That got Cliff's attention: "You mean you have to provide them with an estimated number of worker-days for the use of their camp?"

"That's right."

"Why don't you just inflate that figure?" Harry asked.

"Two reasons: One, the owners multiply that figure by the daily camp cost and add it to our tender price – for comparison with other tenders. Two, should we run into production losses for which we can claim, we would lose the number of days by which we have inflated the true figure."

Cliff nodded and said, "That's out of the question." He gave Harry and Frank a quick look and turned to me. "I think the board committee agrees to give you the go-ahead on this project, Les."

"Thanks."

"Now, let's talk a little about this bonus scheme you have in mind."

I gave them a brief outline of what I had given Phil a week earlier.

"Let me see if I got this right," said Frank. "You intend to pay out an additional ten percent over and above your labor budget, and do this every week with your payroll, regardless whether or not you get an additional ten percent production?"

"That's correct."

"How did you arrive at the ten-percent figure?" said Cliff.

"A calculated guess on my part. Some of my contractor friends have told me that the productivity of union workers increases by about fifteen percent when they work in a non-union environment. Based on that, my ten-percent figure seems reasonable."

Cliff nodded and smiled. "I suppose paying out ten percent is reasonable if the savings come to fifteen percent."

"Who will record the daily production of each worker?" Frank wanted to know.

"Each worker will be expected to do that for himself," I said.

"And how is the production split for a team of workers?" Frank continued.

"On a prorated basis, I suppose."

"Who will verify all of this?" Frank persisted.

"Our supervisors."

Cliff asked, "Do you have a project in mind for your first experiment, Les?"

"Yes. We're starting the government research laboratory soon. This project would be ideal."

"What will be your peak workforce on this project?"

"About four-hundred workers."

"Let me get this straight," Frank again. "You will pay out weekly bonuses with your payroll to four hundred workers?"

"Only at the peak of construction."

"Won't that be an enormous amount of extra work for your payroll clerks?"

"We'll probably computerize the calculations."

"Still, they'll have to input the weekly production data for each worker."

"Yes."

"And how will you deal with inflated data, supposing some of your supervisors are in cahoots with your workers?"

"I'm hoping there won't be much of that."

Cliff again: "What bonus do you have in mind for your supervisors?"

"I haven't worked that out yet, Cliff."

Harry spoke up: "Will your workers be working overtime on this project?"

"It's possible – in the last phase of construction."

"That means their tax bracket could reduce this bonus quite substantially."

"I suppose so."

"What are the unions saying to this bonus scheme of yours?" Harry continued.

"I haven't talked to them about it, Harry, but I don't expect them to object. We're paying the workers regardless of their output."

"I think you're wrong, Les. The unions have a determined

philosophy about equality and the protection of their weakest link. *Any* bonus scheme could jeopardize that."

"I'll talk to them before I proceed."

"In any case," said Cliff, "there is a substantial risk of further loss on larger projects, and we'll have to consider that very carefully, Les." I didn't respond. "Give us a few minutes to discuss it, will you?"

Phil and I walked out into the reception lobby, where the receptionist offered us another coffee.

"I thought you were going to support my scheme one-hundred percent, Phil."

"I did."

"You did?'

"Yes. You were providing them with all the answers. You didn't hear me opposing you, did you?"

I didn't respond. I should've been used to Phil's logic by then.

"What do you think they'll decide?" I asked him.

"I don't know, Les. It's hard to read this board committee. I'm continually surprised by their decisions. They sure grilled you, but that doesn't mean anything."

"I could've been a little better prepared, I think – especially in regards to the administration of the scheme."

It took a full fifteen minutes before Cliff joined us. "I'm sorry, Les, but we have to turn you down for the time being. Your scheme is too risky for the project you picked to try it out. But don't let this deter you from thinking of ways and means to improve production." He gave me an empathetic look.

25

Phil Okays an Info Trip

We were experiencing difficulties with some control modules at a government research center, and the owners' engineer who had specified the modules was getting very worried about their delivery. He had chosen a new, unproven product, and, although we were getting assurances from the supplier's local representative that the delivery of the modules would not delay the project, each time a replacement test module arrived on site, it failed the engineer's check procedure.

Ron Trenton, the engineer, phoned me one day: "You have to put more pressure on your supplier, Les."

"Okay, Ron."

I guess he didn't expect that answer. "Threaten them with a claim," he said.

"That won't do."

"Why not?"

"They've told you when you specified the product that it is still in the experimental stage."

"Yes, but they also told me they would have all the bugs out of it long before we complete this project."

"I wouldn't have put too much trust in that assurance, Ron. These high-tech products can take years in the experimental stage."

"So, what's *your* recommendation?"

"I'll talk to Sahib. Maybe he's got an acceptable solution."

"I don't trust Hassib Singh anymore, Les. He's lied to us too many times. I think we should pay a visit to the factory and find out first-hand what the problem is."

"Okay, Ron. I'll talk to Sahib and get back to you."

We had nicknamed Hassib Singh 'Sahib' because he looked and acted like a gentleman. I put a call through to him.

"Sahib, I just talked to Ron Trenton. He's terribly upset over the failure of the last test module. I think he's also upset that he got sucked into specifying an untried product."

"He didn't get *sucked in*, Les. He wanted this new product despite my warning!"

"Well, he's probably very embarrassed over that. But he told me he doesn't want to hear any more lies from you. He wants to speak to the production manager face to face."

"That's fine. I'll take him personally to the factory."

"Where's it located?"

"Somewhere north of San Diego."

"That'll be an expensive trip."

"Expenses are secondary, at this point. Customer relations come first."

"All right, Sahib. I'll let him know."

When I informed Ron of Sahib's decision, he said, "I think you should come with us, Les. After all, you're the one who issued the purchase order."

"I hope you're not trying to blame *me* for this problem, Ron."

"That's the furthest from my mind. I just want you with me in case a decision of authority is required."

"I'll talk to Phil about it."

But Phil was even less enthused about this proposition than I was. "This couldn't come at a worse time, Les. There are just too many projects on the go."

"I know."

"Let's discuss it later, over a drink."

I phoned Sahib again. "Ron wants me along, too, Sahib."

"That's okay by me. I'll pick up your expenses as well."

"I haven't cleared it, yet, with Phil Potter. I'll let you know tomorrow if it's okay with him."

"Sure. I'll phone the production manager to find out what is the best date in his schedule to see him.

That evening, Phil told me that Ron is right. We're the direct-line customer and should be represented in any discussions with the supplier. "Where's this factory located?" he wanted to know.

"I don't have the exact address, Phil. Somewhere north of San Diego."

"Ah. In Silicon Valley, I suppose."

"No, not that far north. Silicon Valley is north of San Jose."

"I hope you don't intend to make this an extended pleasure trip, Les."

"No. We'll be heading back as soon as we have the information we want."

"Are you flying to LA or San Diego?"

"I don't know. Sahib is making the arrangements."

"Who the hell is Sahib?"

"Hassib Singh, the local representative of the supplier. We nicknamed him 'Sahib' because of the way he behaves."

He gave me his I-don't-trust-foreigners-no-matter-how-they-behave look.

"You better leave me a list of instructions for our various projects, just in case an emergency arises."

"Will do."

Next morning, I phoned Sahib and let him know that I would be joining the team.

"Good," he said. "I'll fax you and Ron the itinerary after I make the arrangements."

The meeting with the production manager was scheduled for 10 a.m. on the following Tuesday. So, we flew to San Diego on Monday. Sahib rented a luxury car at the airport, drove us downtown, and checked us into an expensive hotel.

"Let's meet in the lobby at six," said Sahib, "I'll take you to my favorite seafood restaurant."

"Okay."

The restaurant was located in the Coronado district across the San Diego Bay. The menu's specialty was live lobster. Lobster is not high on my list of gourmet foods, and I commented casually that I knew an excellent restaurant in San Francisco that specialized in exotic seafood.

Next morning, we had an early breakfast and headed north, out of town. The drive took about forty-five minutes, and we arrived fifteen minutes early. The receptionist offered us coffees and Danish pastries, to supplement our sumptuous breakfast. We declined.

In less than five minutes, a tall, lanky fellow joined us. "You must be Hassib Singh," he said to Sahib. "My name is Ted Thornton. I'm the production manager."

"Nice to meet you," said Sahib. "This is Ron Trenton, the owners' engineer, and Les Payne, from Belvue Constructors."

We shook hands, and Ted said, "Please follow me." He inserted an ID card in a wall slot and opened a door, which led to a hallway with internal windows looking into small labs and offices filled with testing and computer equipment. His office was located at the end of the hallway. It had two windows looking out on a treed lawn that separated the building from the parking lot. In addition to his desk, tall bookshelf, and credenza, the office was furnished with a large conference table, surrounded by eight leather-covered armchairs, and a water-filled pitcher and eight cut glasses in the middle on a silver tray.

Ron seated himself at the conference table and pulled a sheet with notes and a notepad from his briefcase, as Ted said, "May I suggest a quick tour of the plant before we discuss business, gentlemen?" We readily agreed.

Ted's so-called plant was one huge area filled mainly with assembly lines. The assembly workers, mostly women, were busy adding various components to printed circuit boards. Ted tried his best to explain the process to us, but even Ron struggled to keep up with him.

After an hour, I think we had seen only half of the plant.

Ron was still interested to see more, but Sahib and I were getting visibly bored. Ted noticed this.

"I think you have a pretty good idea of our activities by now, gentlemen. Shall we return to my office?"

But Ron just got interested in a computerized assembly machine. "How reliable is this process?" he asked Ted.

"Very reliable, indeed."

"Then why don't you use more of these machines?"

"They take a long time to set up – that is, write a computer program for. And if one part is missing, the machine sits idle until the part arrives. We only use them when production runs reach numbers in the tens of thousands."

Ron asked a few more questions as Sahib and I pretended polite interest.

Finally, Ted said, "I have made arrangements for lunch in our private dining room. Please follow me, gentlemen."

The private dining room was more like a plush lounge, with upholstered chairs and fancy glass tables. A waiter took our orders for drinks and handed us small menus with three choices for lunch: a fillet mignon in morel sauce, a chicken breast in light curry sauce, and a broiled halibut steak in white wine sauce. I felt like ordering one of each but chose the chicken breast. Sahib ordered the halibut, and Ron and Ted opted for the fillet mignon. The food left nothing to be desired.

After lunch, we decided to have our coffees in Ted's office, since Ron was anxious to get into his list of notes. His first question concerned the failure of the test modules we had received so far.

Ted cleared his throat. "Well, I don't know if you folks realize how many parts go into each module?" He looked from one to the other of us as we shook our heads. "768," he said. We were astounded. "Yes," he continued. "If you care to see it, I'll show you the parts list."

Ron said, "That's unbelievable. But how does that affect

157

the quality of the product?"

"The properties of a number of these parts have to be closely matched, but we're unable to obtain these from one manufacturer – not even from one country! This means, we have to match them ourselves, with a high number of rejects. Failures can occur when the tolerances are only slightly off or mismatched. This can also happen when ambient conditions change, which, we suspect, is the case in your environment, for example."

Ron was unhappy with this explanation. "Tell me, Ted, and please be completely honest with me: when can you guarantee us a bug-free product?"

"Six months; a year, perhaps."

Ron was visibly shaken. His voice started to fail him. He looked at Sahib with accusing eyes. "Why were you lying to us all this time?"

Sahib shrugged uncomfortably. "I just passed on messages from our sales manager."

Ted spoke up. "I must say I'm just as baffled. I've told our board before we took this order that this product is not ready for the market."

Ron looked at me. "I think we got what we came for," he said with disgust as he picked up his notes and his notepad.

We thanked Ted for everything when we reached the parking lot and headed back to San Diego.

We arrived at the hotel shortly after three and went straight to the bar to get a drink. Sahib excused himself to go to the washroom. Ron looked glum.

"Cheer up," I said. "It's not the end of the world."

"How can you say that, Les? It is for me! I might as well look for another job."

I felt sorry for him. "We'll think of something, Ron."

A glimmer of hope entered his eyes. "Do you really think so, or are you just being kind?'

"I'm a firm believer in searching, Ron. Seeketh, and thou

shalt find, you know? This philosophy has proven itself successful for me on numerous occasions."

He finished his drink and shook his head. "Where's Sahib? I'd like to throttle him, to be honest."

"Don't blame Sahib too much, Ron. I think he feels worse than we do."

We had to wait another fifteen minutes for Sahib to show up.

"Ted's lunch not agree with you?" I asked him.

"No, no. It was fine. I just talked to my president," he said. "We feel terrible over this development and want to do something about it. We propose to supply you with other control modules – not as advanced as the ones you ordered, but a proven product. We'll replace them free of charge with the ones you ordered as soon as they're bug-free." He turned to me: "We'll also pay for the additional preparations and the replacement costs."

I nodded. I was genuinely impressed. "What do you say to that, Ron?"

Ron was smiling now. "I owe you an apology," he said to Sahib.

Sahib was smiling, too. "I'll tell you what," he beamed, "I'll fly you guys to San Francisco and treat you to that exotic seafood Les was mentioning yesterday. Let's check out and head for the airport."

Sahib checked us into another expensive hotel in San Francisco, and, at 8 p.m., we were relaxing at *my* favorite restaurant.

"What do you recommend here?" asked Ron looking at me.

"Abalone if Sahib can afford it. Otherwise, sand dabs."

"Choose anything you like," said Sahib.

"Do you realize they charge $65 for abalone here?" I asked him.

He whistled but said, "Don't let that stop you, Les."

§

Next morning, another surprise awaited us: There were picket lines at the airport and we couldn't get a flight out. Sahib suggested to us that he should rent a car and drive us to another city. We agreed.

There was a line-up at the rental agency, and Sahib took his place in the queue, while I phoned Phil.

"I should be back late tonight or sometime tomorrow, Phil."

"Where are you now?"

"San Francisco."

"What the hell are you doing in San Francisco? I thought the factory is near San Diego."

"It's a long story. I'll tell you all about it when I get back. We're just in the process of renting a car and driving to another city. There's some strike action at the San Francisco airport and we can't get a flight out of here."

"Did you at least get the information you wanted?"

"Yes. We sure did!"

"Okay. Keep me posted."

"Will do, Phil."

When I returned, Sahib was talking to the rental agent. He pointed to a woman who was busy stuffing some papers into her purse. "She just rented the last car available," he said. "She's driving to Salt Lake City."

"Let's go talk to her."

"Excuse me lady," I addressed her, "I understand you just rented our car."

She gave me an appraising look. "You excuse *me*," she said, "I have a long way to drive."

"Do you mind if we tag along with you? We have to reach another city, because we can't get a flight out of here. We'll take turns driving."

She gave each of us an appraising look. "Could I see your photo ID?"

We handed her our cards. She looked at them, at each of us, and at our carry-ons. "I guess I can take a chance with you.

160

My name is Kay Sothern. I'm a financial analyst," she told us, holding out her hand. We shook hands and followed her to the parking garage.

Sahib offered to take the first turn driving, and he expertly steered his way through San Francisco, while Ron and Kay got better acquainted on the back seat. She told him she had attended a financial analysts' convention in San Francisco and showed him a little, hand-held, financial computer that had been part of the registration package. She said she had not yet figured out how to make proper use of it, and, from then on, the two of them were engrossed in solving the mysteries of its advanced technology.

Sahib and I concentrated on the roads ahead – he with the steering wheel and I with the road map. We were a few miles out of Sacramento when I said to him, "Let's stop at Reno's airport. I want to find out if any flights are available."

"Okay."

"Do you want me to drive for a while?"

"No. I'm all right."

We would have had no difficulty obtaining three flights out of Reno, but Ron and Sahib decided to keep Kay company to Salt Lake City. They actually convinced her that driving alone across the Great Salt Lake Desert is very risky. So, I said my farewells and flew home alone.

26

Phil Accelerates the Revenue

Every year as we approached our fiscal year-end, Phil grew apprehensive and studied our budget expenditures. I poked my head into his office one day and said, "What're you studying so seriously?"

"Come in and sit down, Les. I want to talk to you."

"Let me get a cup of coffee. I'll be right back."

As I sat down in the armchair opposite his desk, he said, "Our revenue will be too low this year."

"Shouldn't be, Phil. Our tenders were very successful."

"Take my word for it."

I didn't respond.

"We'll have to do something," he continued. I waited. He gave me an intensive look. "You'll have to accelerate your deliveries, Les."

"That'll create all kinds of problems, Phil."

"I don't care! I need more revenue."

"How much more revenue?"

"Plenty!"

"There'll be a lot of extra costs involved, Phil. We don't have these costs in our project budgets."

"Les, that's for you to solve." His eyes locked with mine intensively again. "You're good at it," he assured me in a more mellow tone.

"Okay, Phil, you're the boss."

He smiled and turned his attention back to his spreadsheet, and I left his office to put the wheels in motion.

As construction materials, as well as process and control

equipment, started to arrive early on various jobsites, our project managers phoned me regularly to complain: "For heaven's sake, Les. I hope you know what you're doing. You're causing us a lot of extra work trying to protect and store these early shipments. Besides, there'll be extra distribution costs when we move the equipment to the final locations."

"I know," I said.

"Then why do it?"

"Phil needs more revenue in this fiscal year."

"You know that he'll just create a chain reaction, don't you?"

"What do you mean by chain reaction?"

"Well, he's robbing Peter to pay Paul, as it were. He's taking next fiscal year's revenue to subsidize this fiscal year. Next year, he'll have to do the same – and so on. That's what I mean."

"I'll mention it to him, Tom."

And I did, when Phil and I were relaxing over drinks that evening.

"Tom's wrong, you know, Les. Our completion percentages may be much higher next year, and I won't have to worry about the revenue."

A light dawned on me: "Don't tell me you're doing this higher-revenue bit to increase your profit for this fiscal year, Phil."

"What's wrong with that?"

"It won't work. That's what's wrong with it!"

"And why not? Pray tell."

"You know head office's policy with respect to taking profits, Phil. We can take fifty percent after we get certification from the owners that our installation is fifty percent complete; the other fifty percent we're allowed to take when we're one-hundred percent complete."

"I know that, Les. You'll just have to convince the owners that we're fifty percent complete, won't you?"

I shook my head. "You're dreaming, Phil." He just smiled.

In the following month, the complaints from our project managers became more frequent. I also received letters from our process and control equipment suppliers, reminding us that the clock for guarantees has started to run earlier because of the advanced deliveries. This was serious enough for me to have another discussion with Phil.

"You know that we have to issue one-year guarantees to the owners after the projects are completed, Phil, but our suppliers' guarantees will run out six months or more earlier."

"I'm not concerned about that, Les. We seldom have to make use of these guarantees – you know that."

"Nevertheless, Phil, if we try to make use of only one nonexistent guarantee, it could eat up most or all of our profit."

He just shrugged and returned his attention to *The Wall Street Journal*.

My next surprise came from an owners' representative: "Your billing is too high, Les."

"I beg your pardon. We have backup documentation for labor and materials billed, Randy."

"I don't doubt that, Les, but you gave us a cash-flow projection for this project and you're exceeding this. My principals are demanding interest charges on the excess."

"Surely, you're kidding me, Randy."

"No, I'm not, Les."

I headed into Phil's office again, with this information. Phil got angry. "The contract doesn't allow the owners to charge us interest on early deliveries, Les. Read it! Otherwise we could charge them interest on late deliveries." I left his office. There was no use arguing with his logic when he was in a foul mood.

My next surprise was almost a shock. Jake Arbut, an owners'

site manager of another project, phoned me: "Les, I have some bad news for you: Your last progress billing has been rejected by us."

"What! Why?"

"Because it includes process equipment which is stored off-site."

"But there's no room to store it on-site."

"That's neither here nor there, Les. Our specs are quite clear on this issue: We don't pay for materials or equipment unless delivered to our jobsite. Change your billing to exclude this equipment, and we'll approve it."

I headed straight into Phil's office again. I thought it was only fair to let him know that some of his esteemed revenue was disappearing. However, he must have expected this.

"Is the equipment in bonded storage?" he asked.

"I assume so. We're dealing with a very reputable storage company."

"Check it out. If it's bonded, call Jake Arbut and tell him we'll assign ownership to him. That's the equivalent of delivering the equipment to the site."

He never ceased to amaze me. The storage was bonded, and Jake agreed to our proposal. This effectively eliminated one more hurdle. I congratulated Phil on his bright idea when we relaxed over drinks that evening.

"Don't mention it, Les. I've had to solve a few problems that way in my sales career."

In the following week, another owners' project manager called me: "We can't process your last billing, Les."

"What's the problem?"

"Short of funds."

"Don't tell me you can't complete this project."

"No. It isn't that. We've made banking arrangements based on your cash-flow projection. The bank had agreed to advance cash based on your schedule, and your early deliveries are raising hell with that."

"So, what can be done?"

"We keep an imprest account. We could advance you some money from that account, if you're strapped."

"Then why don't you do that?"

"I had to check with you first, because there'll be a finance charge."

"I'll talk to Phil and get back to you."

"Okay, feller."

But Phil wasn't at all impressed with that solution. "For heaven's sake, Les, we don't want a *loan*; we need revenue! And if they don't process our billing, we *lose* revenue! Tell them that!"

I did.

"Sorry, Les. I guess I'll have to be plainer: If we process your billing and don't pay you right away, you'll come after us for interest charges, but if we advance you money from our imprest account, we'll come after you for interest charges. Get my point?"

I sure did. Phil got it, too. And this time, he ran out of solutions.

It seemed to me that I was spending most of my time putting out fires caused by these early deliveries. One day, Tom called again: "More problems, Les."

"What now!" My temper was getting short.

"Some of the equipment that was shipped early had shipping damages, and the carrier has a disclaimer if we don't issue a claim within thirty days."

"Our insurance might cover the damages."

"We've checked on that. The insurance company told us that shipping damages are only covered over and above those paid by the insurance company in due course."

"That's okay, then."

"No, it isn't, Les. The insurance company says, had we followed due course, the carrier would have paid for the damages. Therefore, our insurance is voided."

166

I wasn't even surprised at this. Leave it to insurance companies to find some excuse for not paying a valid claim. When I mentioned this to Phil, he had a pat answer: "Go after the supplier, Les."

"What's the supplier got to do with these damages, Phil?"

"The supplier could have engaged a more responsible carrier, Les. Besides, the supplier wants our business again, in the future, I'm sure."

Well, as all good things must come to an end sometimes, so must all bad things. I was glad when we came to our fiscal year-end and when Phil had obtained his precious, additional revenue. It was late afternoon on a Friday, and I had laboriously completed all my monthly forecasts for head office. I signed them all, walked into Phil's office, and plunked them on his desk.

"Thank God it's Friday, Phil. I've had it for one week. Let's get out of here. I'll buy you a drink."

"Best offer I've had all day," he said as he got up.

I slouched low into my armchair after the waiter had taken our drink order. Phil smiled at me. "You look beat," he said.

"I am."

"Got all your monthly forecasts completed?"

"Yeah."

"Any projects with revenue billings below fifty percent?"

"One, I think."

"That's not bad. That'll give us quite a boost in profit for this fiscal year."

"I'm afraid *not*, Phil."

"His smile disappeared. "Why not?"

"Quite a few of our installation-completion percentages are *below* fifty percent, even though the billing percentages are well *above* fifty percent."

"Didn't you check off the fifty-percent-complete boxes in your monthly forecast reports?"

"How could I? We don't have the owners' certification for that."

"Head office will never know the difference."

"Well, I'm not going to take a chance on that, Phil. They may just get it into their noggins to audit us."

"They haven't done that in quite a while."

"They might do it anytime, though. I'm not risking my job and reputation over a few lousy bucks of profit, Phil. I won't do it!"

There was a silence between us for a long while. He gave me a mean look and never took his eyes off me.

Finally, he said, "I don't want you to say any more to me this week, Les."

"Fine."

I got up and walked out, leaving an unhappy man and an unfinished drink behind.

27

Phil Gets Desperate

All too often, when work is scarce and competition is stiff, business people are driven to desperate moves. This shouldn't happen if people realize that lean years may lie ahead and make an allowance for them. It shouldn't happen, but it does. And Phil was no exception. Every year when he updated his five-year budget, he looked at it with rosy glasses, and he never allowed a contingency for potential lean years. I kept reminding him of this, but all he said was, "Don't be pessimistic, Les."

Well, we eventually met up with one of those lean years, and Phil was visibly squirming, especially when we started to submit tenders with zero percent profit, to make ourselves more competitive. We knew that if anything would go wrong with a project that had no allowance for profit, the loss could only be covered from past or future profits, and Phil disliked that intensely.

Under such circumstances, we were preparing an estimate for a federal government research facility and test laboratory, and I had given Phil my risk analysis to be submitted to head office, and he called me on the intercom and asked me to come and see him. I suspected that he wanted to criticize my risk analysis, so I poured myself a fresh cup of coffee before proceeding to his office.

"Les," he said, with his warm, win-you-over smile, "I hope you fully appreciate how important it is to us to land this project."

"Oh, I do, Phil."

169

"Good." His smile was still there. "Then you also appreciate the importance of cutting costs wherever possible."

"I sure do, Phil."

"Very good." His smile broadened a little. "Then will you promise me you'll have another look at your risk analysis with more objective eyes?"

"I don't mind checking it over, Phil. Do you have anything particular in mind?"

"Yes. In your labor-assessment section," he flipped through the pages, "you make some statement to the effect that it is customary, for this type of project, to increase the standard labor units by thirty percent." He looked at me with a frown.

"Yeah, so?"

"So, that's subjective, not objective. Isn't it?"

"For heaven's sake, Phil. The entire estimate is more or less subjective as far as labor is concerned. We're preparing the estimate from past experiences."

"We haven't had much experience with this type of project, Les. In fact, I think we've had no experience at all, and that's my point."

"Perhaps not in this company, Phil, but we have supervisors and project managers who've had experience with this type of project, working for other companies."

"That's neither here nor there, Les. Other companies were probably less efficient than this company."

"I doubt it."

"In any case, it's no use portraying a negative attitude to head office on anything so subjective. You know how easily they spook – they will very likely assume that this estimate is for real."

"But head office depends on me to give them a fair assessment of the risks, to the best of my ability. And, in this case, I'm letting them know that the labor expenditure can end up thirty percent above the norm, and we're allowing for that."

His smile disappeared. "What's the estimated completion

date for this project, Les?"

"Three years from contract award."

"There you have it. A lot can happen in three years. I'm sure construction will be booming again. What I'm trying to say is, supposing the labor budget does run over by thirty percent, the effect of that will not be felt until the third year. By then, the profit of more lucrative projects can cover the loss, and everyone, including head office, will be happy." His smile reappeared. "In the meantime, we end up with a major construction project that will assure our survival. Get my point?"

I sure did. It was hard to argue with Phil's logic. In these circumstances, he played out the role of a benevolent dictator, a godfather. And anyone opposing him was portrayed to be a wrongdoer.

"Phil, I know you have the survival of this division at heart, and I don't disagree with that, but I hate to deceive head office. They depend on me to give them an honest opinion, and my opinion, in this case, is that the normal labor budget requires a thirty-percent boost. I'm not going to alter that." His smile disappeared, and he gave me a mean look. "However," I continued, "you still have two other choices." He looked hopeful and gave me an expectant raise of his eyebrows. "You can alter and sign the risk analysis yourself and claim I was too sick to complete it, or you can leave it as it is and explain to the board committee that, in your opinion, my labor assessment is too subjective and too liberal and recommend a lower budget be used."

He obviously didn't like these choices and looked unhappy. It was one thing to take a chance when someone else's neck was on the line, but it was quite a different matter when he had to stick out his own neck.

"I would prefer not to even mention the potential thirty percent labor loss, Les."

"Well, there's your answer, Phil. You're stuck with the first alternative, I'm afraid."

He looked even unhappier. "I don't think head office has as much confidence in my risk analysis as in yours, Les."

"Well, think about what you want to do and let me know." I got up and walked back to my office.

Phil didn't mention the subject again until we were invited to attend a board committee meeting. "I sent in your risk analysis, Les, with a letter from me attached, pointing out that your recommended labor budget is too high in our present economic environment. We'll just have to try to improve our production."

So, he managed to toss the ball back into my court: Production was my responsibility; he would probably take the position that I'm trying to make my task easier by increasing the budget rather than to become more inventive increasing production. Well done, Phil.

A week later, Phil and I were sitting in the big boardroom at head office, with Cliff Jensen, Jack Osborn, and Harry Linquist. The three board committee members had just finished scanning my risk analysis, and Cliff looked at Phil.

"Give us your explanation, Phil, why you disagree with Les on his proposed labor-budget adjustment."

Phil cleared his throat. He hadn't expected to be on the hot seat quite so soon. "Well, it's quite simple, really. *Any* labor budget is subjective, gentlemen. And right now, we're facing a tough economy, and even tougher competition. I think we need to apply ourselves a little more, tighten our belts, as it were, become more creative – inventive, if you like – improve our production. If we don't do it, our competition will, and we'll be the eventual loser. That's all."

Everyone's eyes were on Phil. Harry even looked at him admiringly.

Cliff turned to me: "Let's hear your side of it, Les."

"I agree with Phil as far as the labor-budget subjectivity is concerned. I also agree that we're into a tough economy and

172

tough competitive conditions. Furthermore, I agree with Phil that we must endeavor to improve production. In fact, we must always endeavor to do so, and we do. Where Phil and I differ is in our analysis of risk. We have been improving our productivity steadily, and our normal labor units have been adjusted accordingly. That means, projects like this one will also have lower labor budgets – albeit, thirty percent higher than the norm. I can point to statistical records to show that this type of project's labor cost ends up thirty percent higher than normal. To allow less on the speculation that production can be further improved is too risky, in my opinion."

This time, all eyes were on me, and Jack Osborn gave me an admiring look. He turned to Cliff and said, "I agree with Les."

The committee members had a few more questions on other parts of my risk analysis. Then, Cliff excused us and requested that we wait in the reception lobby.

Phil sat down and picked up *The Wall Street Journal*. I asked the receptionist to please get me another coffee. While she was out of the room, I said, "You presented some valid arguments, Phil."

"Hmm-hmm. Nevertheless, I think they'll prefer your argument."

"Why would that be?"

"Because they're not risk-takers, Les. Think about it. They never make a move without those damn risk analyses. I know risk analyses are necessary, but I've come to hate them already." He returned his attention to the newspaper.

I felt somewhat similar. My neck was always out a mile. Whenever I made a wrong assessment, Cliff would be upset with me for not doing a better job of anticipation, and losing our expected profit, and if I tried to be more accurate in my assessment, Phil would be upset with me for over-pricing budgets and losing us a needed project. There seldom seemed to be a happy medium.

After half an hour, Cliff came out and asked us to step back into the boardroom once more. When we were settled, he said, "The committee is not unanimous on this matter. Do I understand correctly that the labor portion of the total budget will be about twenty percent, Les?"

"About that."

"So, if the labor budget includes this thirty-percent adjustment you're proposing, this factor would amount to approximately five percent of the total budget?"

"Yes."

He turned to Phil: "Were you going to allow the usual five percent profit on this project?"

Phil couldn't very well say "no," after his recommendation to eliminate the labor-production factor. He said, "Yes."

"Okay. Here's as far as we're willing to go, fellers. Allow the labor-production factor and eliminate the profit. If Phil is right, Les, you'll save the labor-production factor, and he's got his profit, and, if he's wrong, he'll have to forego his profit. But we want you to make a special effort to save the thirty percent. Is that understood?" He gave me a searching look. I nodded. Then he looked at Phil. Phil nodded also.

"Okay, fellers. Good luck!"

On the way to the airport, Phil said, "I'll kick you in the shins if we lose this project, Les. I was going to submit the tender with zero percent profit in any case."

"Very risky to do both, Phil – cut the profit as well as the labor-production factor. I think this is the best solution."

Well, we lost the project, and the difference between our and the low bidder's tender was the budget amount of the labor-production factor. So much for trying to be right! My shins are still sore.

28

Phil Insists on Double-Dipping

Construction owners are always on the lookout for a contractor's double-dippings, especially if an all-inclusive labor rate for extra work has been negotiated at the outset of construction. In the latter case, double-dippings may occur when costs for extra work are being processed via a computer program. The computer is normally programmed to utilize a labor rate with a standard labor burden, with charges for supervision, hand tools, consumables, travel and subsistence expenses, overheads, profit, and so on, added separately. Thus, if a labor rate is used that includes these items, it can happen inadvertently that these additional items are priced out again. An owners' representative who is charged with checking the pricing of extra work usually catches these mistakes and demands an adjustment.

Some so-called double-dippings may be contentious, though, and we ran into one of these on a project that required a claim upon completion. Whenever I ran into a contentious issue that could affect a business relationship, I quickly involved Phil. In this case, I called him on the intercom and asked to see him for a few minutes.

As I settled myself in an armchair in his office, he said, "What's up?"

"Ronald Sharpe is objecting to our method of pricing the claim we have submitted last week." Ronald Sharpe was the owners' project manager.

"What's he objecting to?"

"Double-dipping."

"So, what else is new?"

175

"We're disagreeing with him."

Phil looked up sharply. Normally, the owners' case against double dipping is cut and dried. "What are the details?" he wanted to know.

"We've added a charge for bank interest to our claim, since the costs have been accumulating throughout construction. Ron says that we're already being liberally rewarded by their profit allowance, and the interest charge amounts to double dipping. Therefore, he's disallowing it."

"Owners are in the habit of disallowing interest charges, Les."

"Yes, but this is different. He says that interest charges and profit charges are mutually exclusive and, therefore, amount to double-dipping."

"Is he serious?"

"Yes."

"How do we establish our interest charges?"

"It depends on the circumstances and the bank rate. For our tenders, we go on the assumption that the weekly payroll is financed for about one and a half months, because we don't get reimbursed until the end of the second month. For construction materials, we pay our suppliers on the fifteenth of the month following the invoice date; again, we get reimbursed at the end of that month, so we only finance materials for half a month. And the owners' holdback on our billings, usually ten percent, is accumulating progressively over the construction period and paid out forty-five days after completion. The total finance charge is usually just over one percent of the tender price. But it's about two percent on this claim, because the costs have been accumulating over a longer period."

He nodded. "And how does Mr. Sharpe conclude that we should pay for these interest expenses out of our profit allowance?"

"I don't quite understand his theory on that point, Phil. I thought since you're more into company budgeting and financing, you might want to get this from him first-hand. I could set up a lunch meeting with him."

"Do that, Les."

Ronald Sharpe agreed to meet us for lunch on the following Tuesday at the club. "Call me Ron," he said to Phil as they shook hands. We ordered our drinks and talked about a few general things, like the upcoming elections.

I waited till after we ate and then said, "Ron, Phil is very much interested to hear about your theory with respect to interest and profit being mutually exclusive."

"Ah, yes. Well, it has to do with the purpose for profit. To my mind, if we set aside the risk element, profit should provide a company's shareholders – the owners of the company – with a decent return on their investment." He raised his eyebrows and looked at Phil. Phil nodded in agreement.

Ron continued, "The reason for the investment in the first place is to provide the company with the required operating capital, the working capital, to carry on its business." He looked expectantly at Phil. Phil nodded again.

Ron continued, "So, if the shareholders have provided the company with an adequate investment, the company can function properly, from a financial viewpoint, if not, the company must borrow money elsewhere." He looked at Phil again, but Phil didn't react this time. I think a light dawned on him.

Ron said, "A company usually borrows money for some kind of investment rather than to subsidize its working capital. For example, a company may wish to invest in land and buildings, or in production equipment, and this may require more capital than the shareholders have put up. The interest paid on this borrowed capital would be part of the company's overhead. However, if the company is short on working capital and has to borrow money to run its operations, the interest paid on that becomes a chargeable operational expense." He still looked at Phil as he stopped. Phil nodded again. This was more like it, as far as he was concerned.

Ron continued, "In such cases, the company is entitled to be reimbursed for this interest expense, and the shareholders are entitled to less profit because the company had to supplement their investment with borrowed capital." He paused again to give Phil a chance to agree with him, but Phil's face remained expressionless.

Ron turned to me, "In the case of your claim, Les, you're getting the maximum profit allowed by our specifications, just as if your shareholders had put up the required working capital, and you're trying to charge us for interest, just as if your shareholders had put up no working capital *at all*."

He turned back to Phil, "And that's what I call double-dipping, Phil."

Phil sat there with half-closed eyes and a frown on his face. Ron gave him time to think this over. I tried to suppress a smile. I knew from experience that Phil would come up with a logical answer to refute Ron's theory, and I made a bet with myself that it would take him less than three minutes.

I would have lost my bet – Phil took about four minutes to reply: "I must congratulate you, Ron. You're well versed in a company's financial structure, and you're right as far as the normal operations of a company are concerned – excluding the risk element, of course. It gives me a better insight into the construction owners' reluctance to allow contractors' interest charges. However, you're wrong as far as this claim is concerned." Ron gave him an astonished look. Here it comes, I thought.

"Yes," Phil continued. "This claim does not fall into your normal operational category. It is more like the borrowed capital you mentioned for investments, simply because the costs were incurred over the whole construction period, were paid for by us, and still remain unpaid for by you to this date. This is no different than borrowing money for an investment, in this case the claim – totally outside our normal operations. And, please don't tell me the interest charges on that should be part of our overhead. Our overhead budget does not include interest on claim costs that may or may not exist. Under the circumstances, I must insist that you honor our interest charges." He gave Ron an accusing look.

It was Ron's turn to be silent for a while. I couldn't help but admire Phil's logic. It was almost predictable. I have, time and again, admired his ability to wriggle himself out of tough spots.

But just as I started to feel sorry for Ron, he cleared his throat for a reply: "I must caution you about your insistence, Phil." He gave Phil time to absorb this. "My instructions from the owners are quite clear: Do not allow interest charges. If you insist on getting paid for interest, you force me to go over your claim with a fine-toothed comb to find fault in other areas, which, I'm sure, will amount to much more than your piddling amount of interest. I wasn't going to do that, partly because Les and I have enjoyed an excellent relationship over a number of years, but I will do that, if you insist."

He gave Phil time to digest that. Then he said, "Think about it and let me know. I'll have to run – late for another meeting, fellers." He got up and left.

Phil was still silent for a while on our way back to the office. Finally, he said, "What do you think, Les?"

"I think we should drop the interest charges, Phil. Ron is very good to us, allowing all of our other charges."

Phil nodded. "You're right, Les. Let's call him tomorrow and let him know we're withdrawing the interest charges."

29

Phil Hates Unit-Price Contracts

Most of our contracts were as a result of lump-sum tenders, but, occasionally, we were required to submit unit-price tenders. Phil never liked these, because he was afraid that we might not include all costs in our unit prices. Perhaps this was true. When I mentioned to Phil that our electrical department had landed a unit-price contract, he cringed. "Doing what?" he wanted to know.

"All the grounding on a 200-acre construction site. The grounding for all piles and foundations, for all structural steel, and for the process equipment."

"Who issued the contract?"

"Bentall."

He cringed again. "Watch them, Les."

"What are you getting at?"

"They're not much help to subs – too self-centered."

"I don't know about that, Phil. Our electrical department had a contract for temporary power with Bentall a few years ago. They were very good to us. We made money on that contract."

"Probably because you didn't depend on their schedule for your work. This grounding contract will be different, Les."

Well, I had a taste of what was in store for us soon after the site work got started. Because of Phil's warning, I kept a close watch on our production. Every week, the owners certified the number of units we had installed, and we entered these quantities in a special computerized spreadsheet, allowing us to do an immediate comparison to our budget. Already after two weeks, our labor costs were in excess of the budget, and I called our project supervisor to find out the reason for this.

"What's happening out there, Harold? Our labor costs are starting to run over the budget."

"I'm not surprised," he said, "Bentall is falling behind with the foundations. That's creating some stand-by time for us, Les."

"Did you complain to them about this?"

"I did. They told me they're up against unexpected ground conditions. They think they'll resolve this shortly."

When the trend continued a week later, I called Harold again: "We're still losing production, Harold."

"Bentall is still giving me the same story, Les. They tell me to be patient."

"Well, we can't afford to be patient any longer. I think I better have a talk with their project manager."

"Stan Baker. You have his telephone number?"

"Yes."

"Let me know what he says."

"Okay."

I decided to talk to Phil first, over lunch. "We're running into production losses, Phil, at the Bentall site. They've run into unexpected ground conditions, which slowed down their foundation work."

"Have we notified them that this is affecting our production?"

"We have."

"And are we keeping track of our lost production?"

"Sure thing."

"How much does it amount to?"

"It's not critical, but it could eat up our budgeted profit."

"God, I hate these unit-price contracts. I can't remember a single one that ever made me any profit."

"That probably wasn't the fault of the unit-price contract, Phil."

He gave me his don't-disagree-with-me look.

"I mean," I continued, "the same unexpected ground conditions could be experienced on a lump-sum contract. There *is* a difference, though."

He gave me a questioning look.

"We wouldn't know about our production loss quite so soon. In this case, the owners are keeping track of the number of units we install every week, which allows us to make an accurate comparison of our labor expenditure to the budget. That's how we caught this production loss so fast. In a way, this unit-price contract is a blessing in disguise."

Phil nodded. He recognized this benefit. "So, what do you intend to do to stop this loss, Les?'

"I don't know, yet, Phil. One thing is for sure: We can't bring the electricians out every time Bentall has a work slow-down for a few hours." I think I'll have to talk to Bentall's project manager – find out what he'll suggest."

"Let me know what he says."

"I will."

I put a call through to Stan Baker right after lunch. At first, he was annoyed: "For God's sake, Les, you're wasting my valuable time with a relatively minor issue. Have you any idea what major problems I'm facing out here?"

"I'm sorry, Stan. I'm just reluctant to prepare a claim for this loss we're experiencing. I thought you might have an idea how to avoid that."

He was silent for a few seconds. Then he said, much calmer, "Okay, Les. Let me think about it. I'm rather busy today and tomorrow. I'll call you back the day after."

"Thanks, Stan."

"Don't mention it, Les."

True to his word, Stan called me two days later. "We have decided to give you the temporary-power work on this site at cost-plus, Les, providing you won't charge us a higher labor rate than the one you used for the grounding contract. That should take care of your stand-by time nicely."

I couldn't believe my ears. This temporary-power work was at least as extensive as the grounding work. "I don't know what to say, Stan."

"Thanks would do, Les."

"Yeah, thanks, Stan."

"You're welcome. Now do me a favor, Les: Bother me only if it's really important." The line went dead.

Phil and I enjoyed a few drinks together that evening. "I still can't believe it, Phil – Stan's generosity, I mean."

"Unusual for Bentall, I agree."

"I'm sure we'll do very well on this jobsite, Phil, but we'll continue to monitor our production, just in case."

He nodded.

"This loss experience gave me an idea," I continued.

"What's that, Les?"

"Perhaps we should make unit-price contracts of all our lump-sum contracts – internally, I mean. We could detect production losses much faster."

He shook his head. "Wouldn't work, Les. The reason it works well on your grounding contract is because the owners force us into the monitoring mode. In fact, they do it for us. And our workers know that and go along with it."

"I suppose."

As we continued with our weekly monitoring for the next few months, it soon became apparent that we were gaining productivity. I phoned Harold to find out the reason.

"I think our electricians are charging some grounding time to the temporary-power work, Les."

"Gosh! Don't allow that to happen, Harold. Bentall was very generous with us. I don't want to ruin that relationship."

"I think the guys just want to recuperate the time lost in the beginning, Les."

"We can't afford to do that, Harold. I want you to put down the law: Charge only the time it takes to do the temporary-power work. Do I make myself clear?"

"Yes. Say no more."

"Okay."

I mentioned this to Phil; he wasn't at all concerned. "Saves us submitting a claim for the lost time, Les."

Sometimes I wondered about Phil. He always wanted to maximize his precious profit without realizing what potential damage this might do in the long run.

When our grounding contract was completed, we ran out of temporary-power work as well. We ended up with our budgeted profit on the grounding contract, and slightly more than that on the temporary-power work. I was very pleased, but Phil tried to push for more.

"Are you going to submit a claim to Bentall for our early production losses, Les?"

"You've got to be kidding me, Phil."

He had a smile on his face when he looked at me, probably to make me believe he was joking, which I knew darn well he wasn't. He would've been very happy had I told him, "Yes, of course, Phil."

30

Phil Defends Our Low Profit

Once a year, our company would call all of its managers together for a conference and some social functions. Cliff's secretary, Sylvia, usually made all of the arrangements, with Cliff's approval, of course, and she knew how to pick some exotic places.

Phil and I were having lunch at the club when he asked me, "Did you get your notice for the management meeting?"

"It's probably in the pile of correspondence on my desk. I'll get to it this afternoon. Where is it being held this year?"

"Some private beach resort, north of Fort Lauderdale." His reply was less than enthusiastic. I knew he didn't like these meetings – especially the social functions.

"That's an expensive district, as I recall." I was thinking of Boca Raton.

"A waste of time and money, as far as I am concerned."

"Oh, I don't know, Phil. We usually have some pretty good meetings, and a lot of fun."

"Hmm."

"Are they making any special requests of us this time?" I was thinking of the previous year, when they asked us to submit suggestions to expand our market.

"Not that I could see. Perhaps that'll come later. Last year's request was hypocritical, in any case. Remember? When I suggested the elevated railway project, they flatly turned us down."

"Yeah, I remember. Incidentally, I talked to the contractor who ended up with that project. He told me it is a piece of cake. He's making nothing but money."

"Doesn't surprise me. Fools!" He meant the board committee who had rejected his proposal.

I phoned Sylvia when I got back from lunch: "What's on the agenda of the management meeting this year, Sylvia?"

"Well, we expect you to arrive on Sunday. We'll have a reception Sunday evening. Monday morning, breakfast from eight till nine, and an interpersonal relationship seminar from nine till one. The afternoon is free. Tuesday morning, breakfast again from eight till nine, and a meeting to discuss company concerns from nine till one. The afternoon is free. Wednesday morning, breakfast from eight till nine, and year-end performance and budget projections of our various divisions from nine till one. The afternoon is free again. Thursday, all day, a golf tournament, and a shopping trip to Boca Raton for the non-golfers. Friday, beach activities all day. Bring bathing trunks. For Saturday, we're planning a dinner cruise, starting mid-afternoon. Bring lots of money. You can gamble ten miles out. Make your travel plans to return on Sunday, unless you want to stay longer at your expense."

"Thanks, Sylvia."

"Don't mention it. Hang on a moment. Cliff wants a word with you." She switched me to Cliff's line.

"How are you, Les?"

"Fine. And you?"

"Fine, too. Listen, could you prepare yourself to say a few words at the management meeting on construction claims?"

"That's a big subject, Cliff. How much time do I have?"

"Focus on delay claims. We're allowing you half an hour."

"That's hardly enough. What do you want me to cover in half an hour?"

"Don't go into the details. Cover the highlights – some cautionary tips and how to reduce claims."

"I'll try my best."

"Good. See you in Florida."

§

Phil and I arrived in Fort Lauderdale just after noon on Sunday. We rented a car at the airport and drove north. By two o'clock, we were settled into our rooms at the private-beach resort. Phil asked me to meet him again at three o'clock to drive around in search for a secluded watering hole. He wanted some privacy, he said. I just had enough time to unpack, take a shower, and change into lighter clothing.

We found an ideal place called Blackbeard's Oasis, about five miles from the resort. We went in and seated ourselves on both sides of the bar corner. Phil ordered his usual double martini, and I opted for Southern Comfort on the rocks with a lemon twist.

Phil looked at me and shook his head. "Too many of those will give you a headache," he said.

"I won't have too many, then."

"Did you finish your notes on the claims seminar?" He had seen me making notes on the plane.

"It's not a seminar, Phil. Cliff just wants me to say a few words – cautionary tips on how to reduce claims, as he put it."

"Why would he ask for that at this particular meeting?"

"I don't know. Perhaps it fits into his agenda."

"Or perhaps he's trying to send us a message."

"What message?"

"Increase your profit or cash in on claims."

"C'mon, Phil. Cliff's not like that."

"Hmm." He stared into his martini glass.

"How come you're so morose?" I said.

"I hate coming to these meetings even when we have a decent profit. You know how mean these managers are in their criticism."

"Under our economic conditions, *any* profit is a feather in our caps, Phil."

"Tell that to the other managers." Belvue's managers raked poor producers over the coals, regardless of the excuses.

"I will."

187

I enjoyed chatting to our various managers at the reception on Sunday evening. It gave me a good feel for what was happening in our company. What amazed me was how well some of the divisions were doing compared to ours. I thought that economic conditions were poor nation-wide – apparently not. Phil never showed up. I think he considered these idle talks beneath him.

After the reception, a number of us decided to have a late supper – a mistake on my part: It gave me a restless night.

Next morning, we listened to an expert explaining to us how to get along with each other. He called it *interpersonal skills*. Phil and I were glad when the session was over. We headed straight for our *secluded* watering hole.

"How was the reception, last night?" he asked me.

"Okay. I found out that some of the other divisions were having an exceptional year. Three managers told me they've had profits over a million dollars."

"Beats me how they do it," said Phil. "They've got nothing better than we have."

"Perhaps they've had some exceptional opportunities, Phil." He didn't reply to that.

"There's an astronautical museum around here that I wouldn't mind visiting," he said.

"You mean aeronautical?"

"No, astronautical."

"That may be close to Cape Canaveral. Too far north for a short-day trip, Phil."

"I'll find out where it's located." This time, I didn't reply.

Next morning, Cliff chaired an open forum on company concerns. A number of managers brought up some serious concerns, and it seemed that the discussions on proposed resolutions would never end.

Finally, past twelve o'clock, Cliff said, "I'm going to ask

Les to give us some tips on dealing with delay claims. Les?"

I hadn't expected to be called on at all anymore. Pulling my folded notepaper out of my pocket, I said, "I'm sure most of you are familiar with what I'm going to say, but please don't hesitate to interrupt me if you want to have a point clarified." I paused for a moment. "My first piece of advice is, monitor your production closely. This may sound elementary, but you'd be surprised to find out how few times this is done properly. And, when your production drops, determine immediately who's at fault, and notify this party. Along with the notification, you should provide the details of the cause and, if possible, the effect – that is, the extent of the damage. Furthermore, if you have already initiated an action to mitigate the damages, mention that as well in your notification." I paused again.

One manager asked, "How would you mitigate the damages?"

"That depends on the circumstances," I said. "Sometimes it's possible to shift crews to other areas; sometimes you can send crews to other projects; and sometimes you may have to lay off crews. These are three examples of mitigating actions. The main point is, demonstrate to the party at fault that you are thinking about and are willing to mitigate the damages. Next, try to settle the additional costs for the damages right away, rather than wait until construction is completed. You have more leverage during construction. Furthermore, if you wait to the end of construction, you may have a number of claim causes, which makes compensation more distasteful. And, if immediate settlement is impossible, keep an accurate record of the claim cause, the damages, and the mitigating actions." I looked around for a moment. "Also, keep monitoring your production to catch other claim causes, in which case, the same actions are repeated. However, at all times, remember the business-relations angle. You'll most likely want to do business again with the guilty party, so stay on a good footing and issue a likewise reminder to that party.

Any questions?"

"Could you expand a little on the business-relations angle, Les?" said Cliff.

"Sure thing. The first object to remember in business relations is fairness. If you want the other party to be fair with you – to reimburse you for your loss in the case of a claim – you must be fair as well – in your assessment of the loss. Often, the other party may have budget restrictions and can't reimburse you properly. In such cases, you may wish to negotiate future business considerations. Try to be creative. Another thing to remember in business relations is to maintain a friendly attitude at all times. Keep in mind that people will do more for you if they like you. Any other questions?" There were none.

Cliff thanked me as I sat down. No applause.

When we relaxed at our secluded watering hole, Phil said, "That was quite a presentation you gave them."

"I could've filled in more details, but Cliff only wanted the highlights."

"They're probably lost on them even at that."

"Cliff must have had something in mind when he asked me to say a few words on claims."

"Sure. He wants to reduce frivolous and ill-prepared claims. That's what."

"You could be right. How about taking a run down to Fort Lauderdale?"

"What's in Fort Lauderdale?"

"I don't know. I thought we should have a look around. I hear they have a pretty good nautical museum."

"I'm not interested in any-old museum, Les. I mentioned the astronautical museum the other day because I'm interested in astronautics. Incidentally, the astronautical museum does exist, but it is too far from here to drive back and forth in one day."

Suits me, I thought. I didn't feel like driving all day.

§

Next morning, we got into the financial results and forecasts of our various divisions. As much as the managers tried to help each other during our session on company concerns, the opposite was happening on this day. Most managers leveled severe criticism against other divisions, and the food for that criticism came from the financial statements and budget forecasts. All morning, each division manager had to endure his peers' flak and so-called constructive comments. Tempers were flying high, and, at one point, I thought a fistfight might develop, but Cliff stopped it just in time.

At noon, it was my turn – I was last.

"Profit is a little low this year, eh Les?"

"Yeah. We've had a tough economy in our area, and even tougher competition, I might add."

"Couldn't tell that by your revenue, Les. Your revenue seems to be right up there."

"That's just the problem," said another manager. "The revenue is way too high for the profit – any little thing that goes wrong will turn the profit into a loss. Dangerous position to be in."

That did it for Phil. "Now hold on," he said, "you should dig a little deeper before you shoot your mouth off."

"What's that supposed to mean? You think we can't read financial statements? Gee!"

"I mean financial statements don't show everything."

"Like what?"

"Like the profit we should've been able to take if it weren't for a stupid company policy."

"Now *you* hold on, mister. Company policy applies to us all, not just *you*."

"But we have a number of projects with revenue well over fifty percent on which we were not allowed to take any profit. Do any of you have that?"

Silence. "No. I thought not." He closed his notepad and walked out.

191

"He's right, guys," I said. "We have a lot of latent profit. Might even make the million-dollar club, next year. What do you say to that?" And, with that comment, I, too, closed my notepad and followed Phil.

Phil and I were sipping our drinks in silence at Blackbeard's. After a while, Phil said, "I'm heading back, Les."

I thought about my own interests in the next few days. The dinner cruise didn't turn me on. I'm not the casino-gambler type. The beach games interested me even less, and my golf game was too rusty to join the tournament. However, the company had engaged a pro to tune up rusty golfers.

"I'm not going to join the golf tournament, tomorrow" I said, "but I planned to take some lessons."

"Why take lessons if you're not going to golf?" – Phil's logic again.

"You're right, Phil. Okay, I'll join you. Let's head back. It's more important that we concentrate on next year's profit."

He pulled his cellphone from his pocket and gave Deb, his secretary, instructions to change our flights for an immediate return, and to let him know when the arrangements are made.

31

Phil Shifts His Focus

I awoke one winter Monday morning, and I couldn't make up my mind whether to get up or to stay in bed. Duty prevailed, and I got up. I opened the curtain only to find out that the weather had the same problem: Snow and rain were coming down together.

When I drove to the office, my windshield was soon covered with a sheet of ice, and I had to pull over to wait for the ice to melt, with my defroster on full blast.

Phil was hiding behind *The Wall Street Journal* as I walked past his office. I poured myself a steaming cup of coffee and went back to join him. "Find any good investments?" I said.

"I'm reading the journal for business purposes, Les. It would take much more time to find good investments. In fact, I've decided to do just *that* – spend more time looking for good investments. Up till now, I've spent more than half my day in the business, and my investments were suffering accordingly."

I knew what he was talking about. I've had the same problem.

He looked up at me. "We're getting closer to retirement, Les. It's time we were doing some proper planning."

He had five or six years on me, and I think his study of *The Wall Street Journal* was for more than just business purposes. I could probably learn a lot from him as far as investments were concerned.

"Why don't we compare notes on investments, Phil?"

"Let's do that," he said, with his nose still in the journal. I got up and went back to my office.

§

We started comparing notes at lunch. I decided to appeal to Phil's ego – get him into a pedantic mood, as it were. "What beats me, Phil, is how a person can ever outperform a stock index, like the Dow Jones industrial average."

Phil smiled. "By not buying all the losers included in the index – by picking the right stocks, that's how."

"You make it sound easy."

"Well, it's not easy, but it can be done."

"And what do you look for to pick the *right* stocks?"

He looked at me for a few seconds. I think he was trying to decide if my suggestion to compare notes might be one-sided. I gave him a look of casual attention. Finally, he said, "My first interest is always in the company's products. If the products aren't popular, there won't be much of a profit either. Then, I do some research on the company's management. If the company is mismanaged, even good products won't help much. Good management is often reflected in the company's financial picture: for example, the debt-to-equity ratio, the return on equity, overvalued assets in the balance sheet, the dividend payment record, the earnings-growth record, the cash-flow record, and so on."

He paused for a while. "I also check if the company pays exorbitant salaries to its managers and executives – that can really drain away profits. The best policy is the one in use at Belvue. As you know, our basic salaries are fairly low but are enhanced by bonuses in proportion to our profit. This is a fair way of remuneration – except when profits are postponed, which happened at our last fiscal year."

He paused again. "Next, I check on how the company fares in the market – the price-to-earnings ratio, the price-to-book ratio, and so on. Of course, the market can be seriously wrong about what I call the 'fair value' of a company. For each potential company in which I intend to invest some money, I work out this fair value, and I buy in when the market pushes the price substantially below my fair value. Conversely, I sell the shares when the market pushes the price above my fair value. And, each year, I re-establish all my fair values." He smiled at me.

"Do you mean to tell me that you go through this process for every company in which you may wish to invest money?"

"Sure do. That's why, when I told you earlier I've been neglecting my investments, I've decided to shift my focus. You cannot expect your investments to perform for you unless you go through the process I've just outlined, Les."

During the following week, I couldn't get Phil's comments out of my mind. No wonder my investments were barely mediocre. At best, I had been using a potluck approach and, at worst, an invitation for disaster. Sure, I was giving Belvue added value every day, but I was doing this at the expense of my future, financial health. I came to the conclusion that Phil was right and that I should ask him for more details. I liked his astute approach to evaluating companies.

The following Friday evening, Phil and I enjoyed a couple of drinks together after work.

"What you've explained to me about stock picking the other day, Phil, still seems to me a pretty complicated affair. Couldn't a person hire an investment manager to do that for him?"

"You could if you had enough money to invest. Most investment managers don't want to manage small, segregated portfolios."

"What do they consider to be a small portfolio?"

"That depends on the investment manager. Some will go as low as three million, but the better ones will take nothing less than five million."

"That lets me out, I'm afraid. How about mutual funds?"

"Most investors use mutual funds because they have only a few hundred thousand to invest, but I don't like them."

"What's wrong with mutual funds?"

"Too expensive, for one thing. For another, mutual funds are usually too large to be flexible enough for my liking. Their buy and sell orders may not be covered quickly enough at the desired price. Besides, I don't like their scattergun approach to picking stocks. Remember what I told you about my fair-value picks. I'm only looking at about twenty-five different companies to pick for my portfolio. It's not hard, Les. It just takes a little time."

During the following week, I spent some time in a little mining town, where we were involved in a nickel-processing plant. At the time, the town was occupied only in moderate activities, but the town folks were quite excited about their future prospects. One such prospect involved the huge coal deposits in the area and a giant German gas producing company that had expressed an interest to use its special process to convert the coal to gas and pipe the gas to some major urban centers. When this happens, folks were saying, prices of real estate in the area could easily quadruple.

I wasted no time to phone Phil with this news. "Perhaps we should consider buying some real estate around here, Phil," I said.

"I'm not interested in real estate, and neither should you be, Les."

I felt like Phil had dumped a pail of cold water on a red-hot idea. "It sounds like a sure bet to me, Phil."

"Real estate speculations always sound like sure bets, but, many times, they turn out to be flops. Some friends of mine who had made millions out of real estate are now stone-broke. Take my word for it, Les, stay away from real estate."

"I don't know, Phil. My own house has appreciated quite a lot over the years."

"Has its market price ever been higher?"

"Yes. About five years back, the price was almost double of today's price."

"That should tell you *something*. In any case, real estate, *per se,* is not like a factory that produces salable products. Real estate is too dependent on the whims of speculators and on potential inflation. There are a lot of ghost towns in America with valueless real estate in them. My advice to you is: Stick to undervalued companies."

I thanked him for his advice and hung up, but the low prices of the local real estate were still buzzing around in my mind for some time to come.

Two weeks later, Phil and I were having our lunch at the club. I never mentioned my real estate aspirations again, but I was hoping Phil would be inclined to clear up another couple of things that were bothering me.

"Do you include any foreign companies in your portfolio, Phil?"

"I used to, but I didn't like the confusion caused by the currency exchange."

"You could have hedged the currency."

"Too much bother. I can find all the companies I want in our American markets. Besides, quite a few American companies have world-wide operations."

"I own shares in a couple of Canadian companies."

"Whatever turns you on, Les."

I was silent for a few minutes. Then, I said, "There's one thing that puzzles me, Phil. Perhaps you can clear it up for me."

"What's that?"

"Ever since you mentioned the price-to-earnings ratio to me, I've been paying some attention to it, and I noticed that some companies have unusual high ratios. Why's that?"

"Mostly, because investors drive up the market price for growth companies – sometimes due to hype for a new product. One has to be careful buying stock in such companies. For example, if you buy shares in a company with a P/E of 25, and *if* the company achieves an expected earnings growth of ten percent per year, it would take over seven years to bring the ratio of the price you paid to the earnings at that time down to twelve. But that's a big *if*, Les – keep in mind that the market has irrationally discounted the expected growth. And, if hype over a new product has driven up the company's market price, the fad can disappear as fast as it came." He looked at me with a knowing smile.

"What's the loss ratio for your portfolio, Phil?"

"What do you mean by *loss* ratio?"

"Do any of the companies you pick ever fail?"

"They do, but I try to get out before it happens. That's why monitoring them is so important."

Well, that's the gist of Phil's investment philosophy as he had relayed it to me. Did it improve *my* investments? Perhaps, but I can't be certain – I still continued to pay more attention to my job than to my investments. Sometimes I'm convinced I would have been better off having placed my investments with secure government bonds to, at least, eliminate my loss ratio.